THE EXCAVATIONS AT HELWAN

Frontispiece: First Dynasty porphyry vase

THE EXCAVATIONS
AT HELWAN

*Art and Civilization in the First
and Second Egyptian Dynasties*

----

by ZAKI Y. SAAD

EDITED, AND WITH A FOREWORD, BY J. FRANK AUTRY

UNIVERSITY OF OKLAHOMA PRESS : NORMAN

DT
60
.S18

949

LIBRARY OF CONGRESS CATALOG CARD NUMBER: 68–15689

Copyright 1969 by the University of Oklahoma Press, Publishing
Division of the University. Composed and printed at Norman,
Oklahoma, U.S.A., by the University of Oklahoma Press.
First edition.

108991

Editor's Foreword

To KNOW THE MAN who has made such a remarkable contribution to knowledge about the First and Second Dynasties of ancient Egypt and to have accompanied him on a tour of the excavation sites at Saqqara and Helwan have been exciting events in my life. To have been asked to edit a book giving a general report on the discoveries made at Helwan has been both an honor and a thoroughly enjoyable experience.

Though short in stature, Zaki Y. Saad stands tall among Egyptologists for his contributions to the study of this most ancient cradle of Western civilization. It was my privilege to meet Dr. Saad in 1964, during my fourth visit to Egypt. We met casually at lunch in the home of mutual friends in Cairo, and at first I failed to recognize his name. During coffee following the meal, I suddenly realized that this was the man who had done so much work at Saqqara and Helwan, discovering and recovering whole chunks of history to be fitted into the gigantic jigsaw puzzle that is Egyptian history.

That afternoon was one of the most memorable of my life.

Dr. Saad patiently listened to all my questions and answered them quietly and easily. The rest of the roomful of people simply sat and watched us in amusement.

From that afternoon a close friendship developed. Zaki accompanied me and my wife to every spot we wanted to visit and made the tour doubly rewarding by sharing with us his profound knowledge of ancient times. Until this tour, *Baedeker's Guide to Egypt* had been my only dependable guide to various sites. Thanks to Dr. Saad's knowledge of the locale and of ways to reach the less well known sites, we were able to visit and photograph tombs and temples we might otherwise never have seen. He tirelessly accompanied us everywhere, patiently answering questions that poured out of me, until one day he finally shook his head and said, "Frank, you try to learn too much at one time." I fear that he was right. No sooner had one puzzle been solved for me than many more presented themselves.

In 1966, on a subsequent visit to Egypt, one for which we had made careful plans, Dr. Saad accompanied us from Cairo to Abu Simbel—the "Thousand Miles up the Nile." By this time I had digested all that he had told us on the earlier trip and was ready for more. Now he threw the bait to me—he took us to Helwan and the excavations that are the subject of this book. There he shared with us his own particular enthusiasm: the history of the First and Second Dynasties. Now, after Abu Simbel, Aswan, Luxor, and Abydos, we settled down to Saqqara and Helwan.

Because of his great love for this era, Dr. Saad spent much time and effort explaining and demonstrating what had been discovered and, above all, helping us understand the significance of the discoveries. It was because of my own evolving interest in the beginnings of historic Egypt that Dr. Saad requested me to serve as editor of this book.

My own interest in ancient Egypt developed some thirty years ago, when I began collecting Egyptian postage stamps and wondered what all the monuments were. The *Thousand Miles up the Nile,* by Amelia B. Edwards, the only book on Egyptology in our public library, was my first real taste of the wonders of the past.

During World War II, while serving as a pilot in the Royal Canadian Air Force, I managed to acquire a number of books which had been unavailable in the States, and also to see some parts of the vast Egyptology collection of the British Museum. Upon discharge from service I returned to the United States to finish dental school and at the same time to continue my study of Egypt by corresponding with anyone informed on the subject who would answer my letters. Contacts with various museums proved fruitful, and my library grew—and with it an appreciation for the philosophy of the ancient Egyptian, who so loved the life he led that he wished to continue it unchanged in the hereafter—a contentment not often found in this twentieth century.

My education continued through correspondence with Charles S. Thompson, a former professor living in retirement in Los Angeles. A professional ornithologist, he was also an authority on Egyptology and a stamp expert for the American Philatelic Society, and he was more than well versed in philology. Owing to the assistance of this remarkable man, my studies achieved direction and I began to develop an understanding of all the thousands of years of Egyptian history. Over the years I was to acquire almost all of Professor Thompson's library of Egyptology, which includes a nearly complete collection of the publications of the Egyptian Exploration Society.

During the Korean conflict I was once again in service, this time as a dentist. Stationed in Germany, I had an opportunity to visit the various museums of Europe. Soon afterward I began making regular pilgrimages to Egypt, which were climaxed in 1964 by meeting Dr. Saad and forming the friendship which led to the editing of this book.

J. FRANK AUTRY, D.D.S.

Corsicana, Texas
April 15, 1968

Preface

TWO REPORTS ON THE EXCAVATIONS made at Helwan, near Cairo, Egypt, from 1942 to 1954 have been published to inform archaeologists about our finds. The first of these publications was issued in 1947 and the second in 1950.

Later it was suggested that an independent, general work embodying the results of these excavations should be published so that this early period of ancient Egyptian history might become more widely known. The present volume is the result of that suggestion. This brief work is the first of its kind, for it deals with the art and civilization of this remote era as exemplified in the objects found in the tombs.

I wish to take this opportunity to thank the many friends who so kindly helped me complete the work that made this book possible. I am particularly grateful to Dr. Zaki Iskander, director of the Chemical Laboratory of the Cairo Museum, and his assistants for analyzing some of the material found in the tombs. My thanks also go to my assistant, Mohammad Abd-el-Tawwab-el-Hitta, for his tireless efforts; and to the late Fawzi Ibrahim, architect in the Antiquities Department of the Cairo Museum for the maps and survey he made of the site. Aziz Soryal Atia, director of the Middle East Center in the University of Utah, read the text and made many helpful suggestions.

Finally, my thanks to my good friend Dr. J. Frank Autry, Corsicana, Texas, for his work in editing and preparing the text and illustrations for publication.

ZAKI Y. SAAD

March 15, 1968
Cairo, Egypt

Contents

Illustrations

Figures (drawn from site)

xv

THE EXCAVATIONS AT HELWAN

Introduction

IN 1941, while I was director of the Saqqara excavations for the Department of Antiquities of the Egyptian government, I was appointed chief inspector of the Saqqara district and also of Giza, which included the desert region near Helwan. It was my duty to inspect these regions periodically. It happened that on one of my inspection tours I noticed many fragments of pottery strewed on the ground over a large area southwest of Helwan and north of Ezbit-el-Walda. A study of these fragments convinced me that they were from the same period as those discovered in the tombs in the cemetery of northern Saqqara, which date back to the First Dynasty (3200–2900 B.C.).

The discovery of relics of the First Dynasty is of the greatest importance to Egyptologists because of the meager knowledge we possess about this period. I therefore immediately reported my discovery to the Director-General of the Department of Antiquities, Etienne Drioton, who expressed great interest and joined me in a visit to the area. He soon confirmed my conclusions about its historical period.

The Director-General believed that excavations should begin immediately. Thieves of antiquities had long been at work in the region. Their depredations had resulted in the disappearance of large numbers of priceless objects and damage to many specimens of first-rate historical value. The shards that I found had been scattered about by these robbers, who, when they discovered a tomb, looked only for gold and rare objects, casting aside the pottery as worthless. Of course, to the archaeologist such shards are of great importance as clues to the past. By studying them he can date them and thus date the tombs from which they came.

It was not only plunderers who had mishandled the area. Farmers of the region had stored manure in some of the tombs, and in their visits to the buildings had occasionally come across ancient objects. Authorized dealers in antiquities encouraged the farmers to bring them these objects, for which they paid very little.

At one time and another the site had also been invaded by fanatics who claimed to have supernatural powers to unearth hidden treasure. Such men persuaded local farmers to dig in the area, promising them rich rewards for their labors. Needless to say, their unscientific methods only did the site more harm.

Therefore, to preserve the region from further damage, we proceeded quickly to make plans for excavation. Our work began in July, 1942, and by the end of May, 1954, twelve seasons later, we had excavated 10,258 tombs. A chronology of our work is listed in the table on page 5.

The discovery of such a large number of tombs was an important one in the accumulation of fundamental data about the First and Second Dynasties. Our efforts were re-

	Season	Number of tombs excavated
1	(July 8–October 31, 1942)	735
2	(November 1, 1943–May 31, 1944)	1,632
3	(October 1, 1944–May 31, 1945)	847
4	(October 1, 1945–May 31, 1946)	631
5	(October 1, 1946–May 31, 1947)	825
6	(November 1, 1947–May 31, 1948)	554
7	(October 1, 1948–May 31, 1949)	749
8	(October 1, 1949–May 31, 1950)	1,138
9	(October 1, 1950–May 31, 1951)	1,610
10	(October 1–November 10, 1951)	485
11	(December 11, 1951–May 31, 1952)	904
12	(April 1–May 27, 1954)	148
		10,258

warded by a treasury of rare objects and works of art that clearly reveal advanced stages of art, sculpture, and architecture in the early dynastic periods. Of some of the objects it would be no exaggeration to say that they would equal and even surpass the finest works that can be created today, either by hand or by machine.

Thus, in spite of the earlier depredations to the site, we arrived at splendid scientific results, which are here published and documented in photographs and drawings. It gives me great pleasure to acquaint the reader with the Egypt of five thousand years ago through the excavations at Helwan.

The Kings of the First and Second Dynasties

First Dynasty (*c*. 3200–2980 b.c.)

Mena (Menes)
- Narmer (name in mastaba at Abydos and in tomb at Tarkhan)
- Aha (name in mastabas at Abydos and Saqqara)

Note: The name Mena (Menes) appears on a tablet at Abydos but on no contemporary object. Some Egyptologists believe that Narmer and Aha were two successive kings. Others believe that Narmer and Aha were actually two names for one king (Mena).

Djer (Ity)	(name in mastaba at Abydos)
Djet	(name in mastaba at Abydos)
Udimu (Den)	(name in mastaba at Abydos)
Adjib	(name in mastaba at Abydos)
Smerkhet	(name in mastaba at Abydos)
Qaa (Qa-ay)	(name in mastaba at Abydos)

Second Dynasty (*c*. 2980–2780 b.c.)

Hetep-sekhemui	(tomb unknown)
Nebre	(tomb unknown)
Neterimu	(tomb unknown; sealings of name at Saqqara)
Peribsen	(name in mastaba at Abydos)
Sendji	(tomb unknown)
Kha-sekhem	(tomb uncertain)
Kha-sekhemui	(name in mastaba at Abydos and in temple at Hieraconpolis)

I · *The Site*

THE HELWAN EXCAVATIONS are situated southwest of Maasara and north of Ezbit-el-Walda, about fifteen miles south of Cairo and two miles west of the right bank of the Nile River (Plate 1). The entire region lies northwest of present-day Helwan, at the edge of the Arabian Desert (see map following page 11).

West of the excavations, extending to the banks of the Nile, are fertile, cultivated lands, through which stretches the Cairo–Helwan road. To the east a desert zone separates the necropolis from the Mokattam Hills, at the edge of the Nile Valley.

It appears that from a very early date the vast area west of the Mokattam Hills and south of Cairo was used as a burial place by the Egyptians. This conclusion has been based on the discoveries made by a number of excavation projects in the region. In 1910 Hermann Junker, the Viennese Egyptologist, excavated a cemetery in the neighborhood of Tura. His findings, which were published in 1912, indicated that some of the tombs dated to the First Dynasty.[1]

---

[1] Hermann Junker, *Bericht über die Grabungen auf dem Friedhof in Turah*, Wien Denschriften 56, Vol. I (1912).

In 1920 Paul Bouvier-Lapierre directed an excavation project in the area called El-Omari, north of Helwan. The result was the discovery of a prehistoric settlement, about which reports were published in 1926.[2] Beginning in 1946, work was resumed at this site under the auspices of the Department of Antiquities of the Egyptian government. After two seasons work was halted, to be resumed again for one season toward the end of April, 1951. During the three seasons objects and tombs were discovered which were dated to the prehistoric period.

In 1930 Cairo University sponsored the excavation of a site east of Maadi, a suburb of Cairo, under the supervision of Mustafa Amer. These excavations also revealed settlements and tombs of the prehistoric period. Two books about the Maadi findings were published by Amer and his collaborators, the first in 1932 and the second in 1936.[3]

The ancient Egyptians firmly believed in life after death and planned their tombs with this concept in mind. They selected high places for their cemeteries, since such elevations were usually dry and in no danger of being washed away by the waters that ran down the hills into the valley. Moreover, the Egyptians were evidently aware that the dry atmosphere helped preserve the entombed bodies. According to their religious beliefs, the soul would thus be able to

[2] Paul Bouvier-Lapierre, *Une nouvelle Station (El-Omari) au Nord d'Helwan*, Extrait du Compte Rendu du Congrès International de Geographie (Cairo, 1925).

[3] Oswald Mengin and Mustafa Amer, *The Excavations of the Egyptian University in the Neolithic Site at Maadi*, First Preliminary Report (Season 1930–31), (Cairo, 1932); *ibid.*, Second Preliminary Report (Season 1932), (Cairo, 1936).

recognize the body to which it was destined to return at the time of resurrection.

Later generations of Egyptians took a further step in the preservation of the bodies of their dead when they devised a means of embalming them. The first embalming was performed in the Third Dynasty. From that time onward the Egyptians improved their methods until by the Eighteenth Dynasty they had achieved remarkable skill in the art. Some of the mummies of that dynasty, especially those of kings, are in such well-preserved condition that the hair remains on the scalps and the general features of the faces survive.

The location of this vast burial site has long had great significance for archaeologists endeavoring to discover the sites of prehistoric and early dynastic cities. Junker contended that in the prehistoric period, before the kingdoms of Upper and Lower Egypt were united, there existed a city called Iwnw, or Heliopolis, near the site of present-day Helwan. Junker's theory seems to have been borne out by the excavations at Helwan.[4] This ancient city was the capital of the region for many years, but it began to lose importance during the First Dynasty with the establishment of the new capital at Memphis, on the west bank of the Nile (whose ruins still stand near El-Bedrashen). When Iwnw, or Heliopolis, was abandoned, another city bearing the same name was constructed to the north, where El-Matariya stands today. It grew into a great city, and in time its university became the greatest educational center in Egypt, where famous scholars gathered to pursue their studies.

[4] Zaki Y. Saad, *The Royal Excavations at Saqqara and Helwan* (Cairo, 1941–45), 170.

Many Egyptologists believe that in time the location of the original Iwnw will be discovered. I am convinced that none of the ancient Egyptian cities have entirely vanished. The buildings of the cities were constantly being restored; if a house collapsed, another was built in its place. As a matter of fact, few villages in the country were entirely deserted, as archaeological findings have indicated. Moreover, archaeologists have noted the persistence among present-day villagers of manners and customs known to have been practiced by the ancient Egyptians. The tombs discovered in the cemetery of Saqqara contain many wall reliefs and paintings of scenes that could easily be regarded as a record of the daily life, manners, and customs of present-day Egyptians.

As a village boy I played games which later, as an archaeologist, I discovered were played in ancient Egypt. When, early in my career, I was appointed assistant at Saqqara excavations, I was amazed to discover, in a Fifth Dynasty tomb and in one of the Sixth Dynasty, scenes of small boys playing the same games. Moreover, the expressions and terms used in these games, inscribed in hieroglyphics on the monuments, are, curiously enough, the same as those used in Arabic nowadays. Many other games which I believe are still played in the countryside are shown on the walls of the tombs. This is but one demonstration of the continuity of custom that can be traced through 4,500 years of Egyptian history.[5]

In other words, Egyptian country life has not changed

[5] Zaki Y. Saad, *Annales du Service des Antiquités* (1937), 212–18 ("Khazza Lawizza").

very much, except in language. The basic manners and customs remain essentially unchanged, as do the methods of cultivating the land. The major changes took place in the cities, where the admixture of the conqueror's blood brought about modifications of culture and racial characteristics. The villagers remained comparatively isolated and thus free of foreign influence. Even in language, certain idioms and expressions from ancient Egyptian passed into modern-day spoken Arabic. This was due in the main to a desire to conserve something of the Egyptian rather than to any lack of appropriate expressions in the rich Arabic tongue.

If games and language from ancient Egypt have survived to modern times, it seems a safe assumption that the villages must also have survived, although their names and structures have changed. It also seems probable that the site of old Iwnw may lie beneath one of the still-existing towns somewhere in the area extending from Maadi to Helwan.

What do we know of the origins of Helwan? The Arab historian El-Makrizy wrote: "It is stated that Helwan is the name of one of the Arab leaders—Helwan, son of Babylon, son of Amr, son of Amir-el-Kais, king of Egypt, son of Sabs, son of Zekob, son of Gahob, son of Kahtan. Helwan lived in Syria as chief of the advanced guards in Braha."[6]

The Arab historian El-Kindy says: "The plague spread in Egypt in 70 hegira [A.D 692]. Abd-el-Aziz Ibn Marawan, for this reason, left the city [for the Helwan site], and when the place pleased him, there he resided, keeping his soldiers with him as well as the guards and the policemen. Abd-el-

---

[6] Quoted in W. Reil, *The Sabino-Sulphureous Thermal Springs of Helwan* (Cairo, 1878).

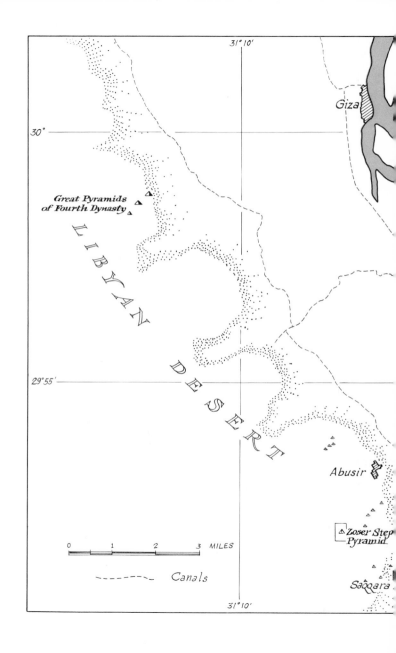

31° 10'

Giza

30°

△
Great Pyramids △
of Fourth Dynasty △

L I B Y A N

29° 55'

D E S E R T

△
△ △

Abusir

△

△ *Zoser Step
Pyramid*

△

Saqqara

0   1   2   3   MILES

- - - - - - -   *Canals*

31° 10'

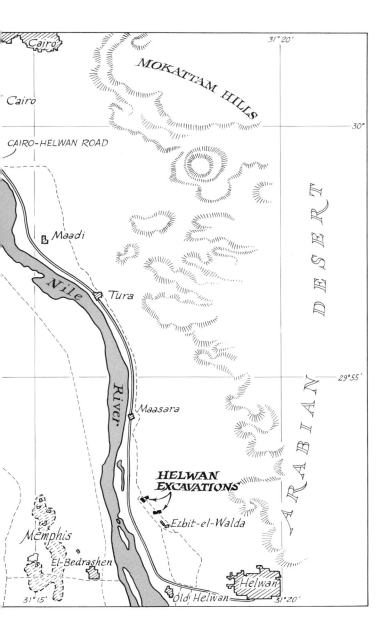

Aziz built there mosques and palaces and brought many people to live in the district. He planted palm trees and vineyards which were the subjects for many poets. Abd-el-Aziz who planted the palm trees ate their fruits with his soldiers. He used to walk always under their shade staying close by the springs."[7]

According to El-Makrizy, when Marawan, the father of Abd-el-Aziz, left Egypt in the month of Rajab, in the year 67 hegira (A.D. 689), Abd-el-Aziz succeeded him as ruler of Egypt. Marawan died in the month of Ramadan, and his son Abd-el-Malik succeeded him as ruler of Syria, leaving Abd-el-Aziz in charge of Egypt. In 86 hegira (A.D. 708) Abd-el-Aziz fell ill and died. His body was transported on the Nile from Helwan to El-Fostat (Old Cairo), where it was buried.[8]

Thus early Arab historians concluded that Helwan had been named for the Arabic leader Helwan, assuming that the city of Helwan had not existed before the arrival of the Arabs. With all due respect to their views, we must seek elsewhere for information about the founding of the city and the origin of its name. For one thing, a Coptic monastery was in existence in the Helwan region before the Arab conquest of Egypt. Furthermore, the Romans knew of the baths at Helwan and visited them, bringing their camels to be treated for skin diseases. It does not seem very likely that, when the plague spread in El-Fostat, Abd-el-Aziz Ibn Marawan deserted it to set up residence in an uninhabited region. It is far more likely that he went to Helwan, which was al-

7 *Ibid.*
8 *Ibid.*

ready a habitable city, and merely improved its buildings and turned it into a more comfortable place to live.

The Coptic monastery which I discovered in Helwan is among the largest ever found in Egypt. The building contained more than sixty-six rooms. The court in the middle of the monastery was divided into several sections. In the north part there was an orchard, and one can still see the holes that were filled with Nile River mud to fertilize the trees. Portions of irrigation aqueducts, which were constructed of burned bricks taken from tombs that had been set on fire, are also still visible. In the south part was a moderate-sized church and a cemetery, in which we found graves containing the bodies of monks. There was also a large reservoir in which the monks stored water. Next to the reservoir was a structure of strange design in which earthenware jars were fitted into holes in the walls resembling pigeonholes. We are not certain of the purpose of this structure; it may have been a swimming pool.

The Arab historians Shaboshty and Abou-Saleh mention that when Abd-el-Aziz arrived at Helwan he resided as a guest in a monastery for a while and afterward ordered the construction of palaces in the neighborhood for permanent residences. This statement confirms the existence of the monastery, which, judging from the pottery and glass fragments found on the site, we have become convinced was of Byzantine origin.

It is certain that the monastery continued to flourish until at least the year 152 hegira (A.D. 774). At the site we found several bronze coins and four gold ones bearing dates ranging from 79 to 152 hegira (A.D. 701 to 774). The bath of Abd-el-Aziz, built in 69 hegira (A.D. 691), was discovered when Helwan was restored in 1872.

The existence of the First Dynasty necropolis, and of even earlier sites, near Helwan, together with the probable existence of the old capital Iwnw in this region, has led me to conclude that the name Helwan was an ancient Egyptian name that passed into Arabic through Coptic. It is also probable that Helwan was a suburb of the old capital Iwnw and was known in those times as Her-Iwnw—that is, the "City above Iwnw." Since most of the old Egyptian place names were adopted by later generations, it is likely that the Arabs changed *Her-Iwnw* to *Helwan.* The change from *r* to *l* is not uncommon in spoken Arabic. Similar changes certainly took place; for instance, Hathor-Nebet, near Old Cairo, named for the goddess Hathor, became Athar-el-Naby in Arabic.

It is such theories as these that offer endless challenge to the archaeologist. Certain it is that the more he explores, provided he works systematically and scientifically, the more he discovers about the land of the Pharaohs. Some of these discoveries will be the subject of the following pages.

II · *The Tombs*

THERE IS NO DOUBT that the Egyptians of the First Dynasty were highly civilized and far advanced in comparison with other peoples of the period. The buildings discovered in the excavations at Helwan are evidence of the degree of excellence they had achieved in architecture by that remote period.

To the ancient Egyptian, his tomb was to be his abode in the other world until the day of resurrection. The Egyptian believed that the other-world life was the real and eternal life and that it was his duty to prepare himself for it by every means. Any negligence in this duty was considered heresy, a falling away from faith in the long and happy life to come, with which one's first life on earth could not compare.

Since his other-world abode was so important to his future life, every Egyptian built a tomb that would befit his rank and social standing. A man of position and wealth built a tomb as large and pretentious as his means allowed. The interior of his tomb consisted of numerous chambers stored with various objects for him to use and enjoy during his life in the other world. The tomb of a poor man might be a simple grave dug in the earth, but his future welfare was not ignored. Vases and other objects for his use were often buried with him.

Tomb 1371 H.2 is a great structure of mud bricks. Among its features is a well-constructed staircase. The first section of stairs, about 3 meters long, runs from west to east and is made up of seven steps, at the end of which is a step 1 square meter in size. From that point seven more steps extend in a southerly direction for a distance of 4 meters. Like the walls, the steps are constructed of mud bricks and are covered with lime whitewash.

A stone portcullis blocks the entrance to a passageway, on each side of which is a magazine, or storeroom. In the magazines were found large-sized pottery granaries, or jars (Plate 2). At the end of the passage is a door blocked by a slab of white limestone. This door leads to the burial chamber, which is paved with three slabs of limestone (Plate 3). The manner in which burial chambers of this period were paved was unknown until the discovery of this tomb. In the northwest corner of the chamber we found the largest pottery jar in our collection; it is also the largest yet recovered from any tomb of this period. It was found broken into numerous fragments and was later restored (Plate 20).

In the debris of the tomb were found several pottery stoppers, some of which bear seal impressions. The stoppers were in poor condition; however, on one of them (Plate 4) we were able to read the name of King Adjib, the sixth king of the First Dynasty (see the list of kings of the First and Second Dynasties, page 6). On another pottery stopper the name of the same king was faintly discernible, and with it was the name of the official to whom the tomb belonged. The name of the official was damaged too severely to be readable.

According to the evidence, this tomb belonged to one of the officials of the reign of King Adjib.[1] The size and structure of the tomb give us an idea of the social position of its owner, who was no doubt an influential person. The tomb had been robbed of its treasures, and nothing was left in it except objects that were of no interest to plunderers.

Tomb 1374 H.2 was in very badly damaged condition. A canal that had been cut through the area had eroded the northeast corner of the mastaba, or superstructure. Moreover, fertilizer dealers (*sabbakhin*) had evidently helped themselves generously to its walls of bricks made from the rich Nile River mud. The remains of the mastaba indicate that the four interior walls were covered with plaster (Plate 5) and that the tomb was surrounded by an outer wall like those around the big tombs discovered at Saqqara.[2]

Leading into this tomb is a staircase running from west to east and ending in the burial chamber, which is built of mud bricks (Plate 6). There are two magazines south of the burial chamber, both on a level higher than that of the chamber floor. The tomb was set on fire at some time, and the walls of the burial chamber, magazines, part of the entrance, and the steps look as though they had been built of burned

[1] Etienne Drioton and Jacques Vandier, *Les Peuples de l'orient Mediter-ranéen: II. l'Égypte* (2d ed., Paris, 1952), 136, 138, 142–43, 147, 150, 159–60, 163–64, 200.

[2] Walter B. Emery, *Excavations at Saqqara: Great Tombs of the First Dynasty* (Cairo, 1949).

bricks.[3] In the western magazine we found some pottery jars. In a hole made by the robbers we found a pottery lamp, probably left behind by the robbers. The lamp is Roman and provides some evidence of the date of the pillage and the fire.

Tomb 785 H.5 is another large structure built of mud bricks. A staircase 900 centimeters long lies west of the burial chamber and ends in a passage. The steps, also of mud bricks, were obviously built with great care (Plate 7). The passage ends in a vestibule, extending from west to east, 250 centimeters long and 120 centimeters wide. North of the passage are two magazines, each provided with a door. On the south wall of the passage is a door leading to the burial chamber, which is about 250 centimeters long, 320 centimeters wide, and 270 centimeters high.

Above the two magazines north of the passage are four smaller ones (Plate 8). The tomb was found in a very poor state of preservation (it had also been damaged by fire following a robbery), and it is not possible to say for certain whether there were similar magazines on the same level. However, it is certain that there were several magazines in the mastaba; four magazines are still standing in the southern part of the superstructure.

The mastaba measures 20 meters from north to south and 12 meters from east to west. There were probably fourteen magazines altogether, constructed in two rows of seven magazines each. The mastaba was surrounded by an outer

[3] Many of the tombs in the Helwan necropolis had been burned. Some fires were doubtless accidental, but others were deliberately set by superstitious robbers to destroy the bodies so that the dead men's souls could not return to identify those who had robbed their tombs.

enclosure wall and was separated from the wall by a passage on all four sides. The staircase begins outside the wall (Plate 9).

In the west side of the southern section of the super-structure is a chapel, built facing the west. This feature was noted in many other First Dynasty tombs in the cemetery of Helwan (Plate 10), and must be considered one of the significant discoveries made about the religion of the Egyptians of this period. These discoveries will be dealt with in greater detail in Chapter VII.

In the chapel we found five pottery offering jars, all of the same type, sunk deep in the ground with only the rims visible. The jars were placed in two rows next to the building (Plate 20). We know that during the Second and Third Dynasties, and even later, an offering table was placed in front of a false door. The table was made of stone. In some cases it bore inscriptions of offerings presented to the soul of the tomb's owner. The five jars in this chapel were evidently filled with offerings to sustain the dead man in the other world, and there is no doubt that this custom preceded the practice of laying an offering table with symbolic offerings in the form of inscriptions or representations.

From all the evidence we concluded that this large tomb must have consisted of three stories. The first story contained the burial chamber, separated by a passage from the two magazines on the north. The second story contained the four magazines above the two in the first story. The third story was formed of the mastaba, together with fourteen maga-zines, the corridor, and the outer wall (Plate 9). The roof of the tomb, the magazines, and the staircase were constructed of huge blocks of timber, which were found burned to cinders and charcoal.

Tomb 423 H.9 is the largest excavated in the area. It is built of mud bricks and has both substructure and super-structure. The substructure includes the burial chamber, two magazines on the north, and two on the south. All the walls are plastered smooth with mud and red wash. Some traces of bright-red paint are still detectable, five thousand years after the tomb's construction.

The substructure was roofed with limestone (Plate 11). The stone roof was intended to protect the tomb from rob-bery; but in spite of this precaution robbers reached the burial chamber by tunneling three passages from outside the wall. Two of the passages are on the west, and the third is on the east. The burial chamber and three magazines were plun-dered. Only one magazine, in the southwest corner, was found intact. In it we discovered pottery and several care-fully made vessels and dishes of alabaster and slate, which testify to the skill of the craftsmen of the period. A clay stop-per on one of the jars bears the name of King Udimu, fifth king of the First Dynasty.

The burial chamber is 410 centimeters long, 210 centimeters wide, and 380 centimeters high. The magazine in the south-west corner is about 145 centimeters long, 95 centimeters wide, and 380 centimeters high. The magazine on the east is about 160 centimeters long, 140 centimeters wide, and 380 centimeters high. The east magazine on the north is about 130 centimeters long, 95 centimeters wide, and 380 centi-meters high, and the west magazine on the north is about the same size. There is no communicating staircase from the surface to the burial chamber. This design was also found in other tombs.

The mastaba of the tomb is rectangular, and all four walls were covered with plaster, many parts of which have been destroyed (Plate 12). The length of the mastaba, from north to south, is 40 meters, and the width, from east to west, is about 25 meters. The walls of the mastaba are 250 centimeters thick.

Around the mastaba is a wall measuring 45 meters north to south and 27 meters from east to west. Between the outer wall and the mastaba is a passage about 100 centimeters wide.

The owner of the tomb provided himself with a wooden funerary bark 12.5 meters long. The remains of the bark were found north of the tomb, facing eastward (Plate 13).

Because of the large dimensions of this tomb and of the site on which it was built, the name of the king inscribed on the stopper, and the boat with which the tomb's owner was provided, we can judge that the owner must have been an official of influence and high social position in the reign of King Udimu.

The tombs described above, all built of mud bricks, are evidence of the high architectural standards of the First Dynasty. Mistakes are rare, in either the lines or the angles of the buildings, and the architects of that remote period obviously possessed skill and taste. Because the tombs were to be the other-world homes of the dead, they must have been designed and built much like the houses in which the Egyptians led their temporal lives. We may therefore assume that the owners of these tombs had fine, comfortable houses, carefully and tastefully constructed.

IN HIS BUILDINGS the Egyptian of the First Dynasty did not use mud bricks alone; he also used stone. Until we came across tombs built of white limestone, it had not been known that stone buildings were erected in the First Dynasty. This discovery provided the key to a puzzle that archaeologists have long tried to solve.

Every visitor to Saqqara is struck by the sight of the Step Pyramid, built for King Zoser in the Third Dynasty. It has long been believed that a stone building of such perfection could not have been the first of its kind and that it must have been the culmination of generations of experimentation in stone architecture. But until the cemetery at Helwan gave up its secrets, examples of earlier efforts in stone had never been found. At Helwan we were fortunate to discover specimens of the achievements of First Dynasty architects— achievements that helped make possible the construction of the Step Pyramid.

We found large tombs designed not for kings but for private individuals with burial chambers built of large blocks of reasonably well cut limestone, together with steps and magazines of the same material (Plate 14). Until these tombs were found, the prevailing theory among Egyptologists was that, except for the limestone tomb of King Kha-sekhemui, the last king of the Second Dynasty, stone buildings were not constructed until the Third Dynasty and that the stones were small, large stones not being used until the Fourth Dynasty. But at Helwan we found the walls of burial chambers built of large slabs of limestone, placed side by side, not in layers. The burial chambers are also paved with stones. Until these tombs were found, the only known use of stone pavement in this period was in the tomb of King Udimu at Abydos, whose burial chamber is paved with granite.[4]

Tomb I H.3, of the First Dynasty, is a very large one. The staircase first runs from west to east and then turns to the south toward the burial chamber. The steps are made of stone, and the walls are built of mud bricks encased in white limestone slabs.

In the walls of the staircase are grooves for portcullises, two of which are still in position. One of the portcullises has four holes in the lower part (Plate 14). At the end of the steps are two magazines, one on each side, cut into the gravel. The burial chamber was also cut into the gravel, and walls made of mud bricks were placed on top and encased in large slabs of white limestone, placed vertically side by side. In the southeast corner of the burial chamber there is a stone slab with two holes at the upper edge (not shown in Plate 14). This was the last slab to be placed in position, and ropes were passed through the holes to lower the block. Small pieces of stone were placed east of the last slab after the block was lowered.

The burial chamber was roofed with huge timber beams covered with wooden planks. Like other tombs at the site, this tomb was also set on fire. The mud-brick walls behind the stone slabs turned red from the fire, making it appear that the walls had been built of burned bricks.

There are very few traces left of the mastaba built around the tomb. The *sabbakhin* removed most of the surface bricks from the site. On the east and west sides of the tomb, and

---

[4] Drioton and Vandier, *Les Peuples de l'orient Mediterranéan: II. l'Égypte,* 152.

extending the length of the tomb, we found rows of holes filled with Nile River mud. The only explanation of this feature is that trees were planted alongside the tomb.

The person who could afford to build such a tomb must have been one of high position. The stones were cut from quarries in the Mokattam Hills. After they were cut and dressed, they had to be transported to the tomb site. All these operations were very difficult and could only have been carried out by a powerful and influential person.

Tomb 40 H.3 (Plate 15) also dates from the First Dynasty. In this tomb the staircase runs from north to south. The steps and walls are built of stone. Two portcullises still stand in their original positions. The burial chamber and the two storerooms on each side of the entrance were first cut into the gravel and then walled with large white limestone blocks, in the same manner as in tomb No. 1 H.3. There are two doors in the passage between the magazines. The stone blocks walling both the burial chamber and the two magazines are reinforced with blocks of the same stone placed on their sides to prevent the standing blocks from falling (Plate 15). The floor of this tomb is paved with small limestone slabs. The last portcullis is broken at the top, and only one hole can be seen in the remaining part. The portcullis behind it has two holes in the lower part.

Both tombs described above were thoroughly plundered. The only items we found were a very few alabaster fragments and broken pottery jars, but from these fragments we were able to date the tomb as belonging to the First Dynasty.

In the debris on the ground around the tombs we came across some interesting and important objects. One, a rectangular piece of faïence in the form of a *serekh* (a rectangular framework supported by paneling, which represents the façade of the palace) bears on both sides the two signs for King Narmer's name, the fish and the spear.[5] These signs are inlaid in black material, which is most likely a glazed pigment made from ground carbon. The piece is 2.6 centimeters long, 2 centimeters wide, and 6 millimeters thick.

A similar piece bears on both faces a hawk and below it the sign denoting the name of King Djer, the third king of the First Dynasty. These decorations are also inlaid in black material.[6]

We found a cylindrical seal made of soapstone, 3 centimeters long and 0.9 centimeter in diameter (Plate 95). On it is incised the figure of a man whose head resembles that of a bird with a long beak. The three fingers on each hand resemble talons. Beside the man are two giraffes facing one another, separated by a tree. In front of the giraffe on the left is the sign of the god Min; above it is the representation of what appears to be a crocodile. Above the giraffe on the right is the representation of a falcon standing on a *serekh* and apparently holding a mace and a shield. The entire group evidently represents the name of King Aha, the second king of the First Dynasty.[7]

We also found several pieces representing emblems of gods. Some pieces of faïence and limestone have the form of the emblem of the god Horus, who is represented by the

[5] Saad, *The Royal Excavations at Saqqara and Helwan*, 165, Fig. 13.

[6] *Ibid.*, 166, Fig. 14.

[7] Walter B. Emery and Zaki Y. Saad, *The Tomb of Hor-Aha* (Cairo, 1939), 38, 74, Plates 20–24.

falcon (Plate 111A to D). One piece of faïence, in the form of a vulture, represents the goddess Nekhbet, of the nome, or district, of Nekhen (El-Kab) (Plate 111E). There are also pieces of faïence and alabaster representing the god Min (Plate 112). More will be said about these discoveries in a later chapter.

All the evidence we found at tombs 1 H.3 and 40 H.3 indicates that they were constructed early in the First Dynasty, which means that the Egyptians were accustomed to using stone in their buildings long before the Third Dynasty.

Changes in architectural style and method took place in the second part of the dynasty, in the reigns of King Udimu and King Adjib, as indicated by our discoveries at tomb 1390 H.2. The burial chamber in this tomb is constructed of large slabs of white limestone. Each slab is 250 centimeters long, 80 centimeters wide, and about 20 centimeters thick. The slabs are placed on their sides in a row, the longer side resting on the ground, the shorter side upward (Plate 16), in contrast to the method used in tombs 1 H.3 and 40 H.3 (Plates 14 and 15). The chamber wall consists of two courses, or rows, of slabs, fitting into one another.

There are two magazines on each side of the burial chamber, and there was no way to reach the south magazines from those on the north except through the burial chamber itself. Thus some kind of door or opening had to be devised in the wall adjoining the magazines. This opening was ingeniously provided in the lower course of slabs; the builder cut the upper slab in such a way that it fit into the wall and the lower course and provided a lintel above the entrance. The lintel was cut straight at the end where it joined the adjacent

28

wall, and the other end was cut at an angle to fit it to the slab beside it (Plate 16). This tomb provides us with a clear example of innovations that were made in stone building during the later part of the First Dynasty. Moreover, these and other discoveries in the Helwan excavations make it possible for us to trace the evolution of architectural design that led to the construction of the Step Pyramid.

Tomb 385 H.4, also of the First Dynasty, is considered among the most important discoveries at Helwan. Except for one magazine, which remained intact, this tomb had also been looted. A descent from the north, cut into the gravel, leads to a flight of steps made of mud bricks. The steps end at the north wall of the burial chamber, and there is no door communicating with the chamber itself. On each side of the steps are two magazines. The rectangular burial chamber was cut into the gravel and then walled with stone slabs on all four sides.

The north and south walls are formed of single blocks of white limestone, each block 4 meters long, 2 meters high, and about 40 centimeters thick. The east and west walls are composed of similar blocks, plus a second block at the south end of each wall, which is 170 centimeters wide, 2 meters high, and about 40 centimeters thick (Plate 17). The extra blocks were added to make the burial chamber longer in one dimension. The chamber measures 522 centimeters from north to south, 4 meters from west to east, and about 425 centimeters from the chamber floor to the ground level.

The ledge on the east side is 130 centimeters wide; that on the west is 60 centimeters wide. On top of the ledges there were probably flat slabs, forming the roof of the chamber.

Since there was no door to the chamber, the roofing slabs must have been set in position after the body was placed in the tomb. The magazines were also roofed, probably with timber beams, and then the entire structure was covered with rubble to the surface level. There is no evidence of a mastaba aboveground.

The magazine on the northeast corner of the tomb is 110 centimeters long, 110 centimeters wide, and 485 centimeters high. In it were found some broken pottery jars and dishes of the type commonly used in the First Dynasty. The adjacent magazine is 125 centimeters long, 105 centimeters wide, and 485 centimeters high. Nothing was left in this magazine.

The magazine on the northwest was found intact. It is 110 centimeters long, 90 centimeters wide, and 350 centimeters high. In it we found layers of ribs and other bones of sacrificial oxen. Below the first layer of bones we found a nicely shaped flint knife 35 centimeters long (Plate 40). Beside the knife were some pottery dishes and two tubular alabaster jars. One jar, slightly damaged, is 23 centimeters tall, 13 centimeters wide at the base, and 105 centimeters in diameter at the mouth. The rim of the jar is 3 centimeters thick. The jar is well-polished both inside and out. The second jar is of poor-quality alabaster, and the workmanship is inferior to that of the first jar.

A sandstorm that began about the time of our discovery of this magazine obliged us to delay clearing it for some days. We photographed the flint knife *in situ* and assumed that there was nothing more to be found. On commencing work again, however, we discovered still deeper in the magazine more layers of bones with two flint knives underneath them

(Plate 41), placed across one another in the form of a pair of scissors (Plate 42). Both knives are intact; one is 44 centimeters long, and the other 41.5 centimeters long. The workmanship is as excellent as that of the first knife we found. The shapes of all three knives are elegant. The two found at the lower level are probably the largest of their kind yet recovered from tombs of this period.[8]

The magazine on the southwest side of the tomb, which had also been plundered, is 1 meter, 30 centimeters long, 90 centimeters wide, and 1 meter, 30 centimeters high. The tomb robbers reached the burial chamber by means of a tunnel on the east side, which was dug straight down from the surface to a point below the ceiling of the tomb. Here the robbers broke through the gravel ledges and the top of the stone block that walled the east side (Plate 17). The fact that most of the tombs were reached in the same way indicates that the roofs of the tombs were still solidly in place at the time they were robbed. In one tomb we found the remains of a robber who was crushed to death under a wall that gave way during the tunneling. The positions of the tunnels indicate clearly that the looters knew the exact positions of the tombs. Since the tombs are of different designs and many of the original superstructures have long since disappeared, it is probable that the looting took place almost immediately after the burial of the tombs' owners.

ONE INTERESTING FEATURE of tomb 385 H.4 is the huge blocks that wall the burial chamber. In previous seasons we had

[8] Cf. Walter B. Emery and Zaki Y. Saad, *The Tomb of Hemaka* (Cairo, 1938), 18, Fig. 5, Plate 1.

come across tombs built of limestone blocks which we had at the time considered to be of extraordinary size; but here we found blocks double the size of the earlier discoveries. They demonstrate the skill the tomb builders had achieved in cutting and dressing the stones, and also the effort required to transport them from the quarries to the tomb site. There were no regular roads or causeways like those that were built at Giza and elsewhere, and the transportation of these great slabs must have been a gigantic task. Presumably the ancients used rollers and sledges for this purpose.

We were not able to identify the owner of this tomb. We can only assume, from its size and the high quality of the workmanship, that the owner must have been an influential person in his time.

Tomb 287 H.6 is one of the largest discovered at the Helwan site. Its mastaba has been almost entirely destroyed; what is left of it indicates that it was built of small limestone blocks and measured 56 meters from north to south and 27 meters from east to west. The east wall was originally encased in well-dressed white blocks. This wall was not perpendicular but was inclined inward, making the top of the mastaba narrower than the base (Fig. 1). The remaining three sides were perpendicular and were protected by a mud-brick wall. The wall protecting the north side was in fairly good condition—in much better condition than the other walls. The mud wall was in turn protected on the outside by larger boulders and unshaped stones.

In the center of the mastaba we found a rectangular shaft walled in a curious manner. The north, east, and west walls of the shaft are built of limestone blocks, undressed and

Figure 1

shaped to resemble mud bricks (Fig. 2 and Plate 18). The south wall is built of large horizontal blocks of white limestone, comparatively well dressed and measuring 4 meters, 50 centimeters long, 1 meter, 10 centimeters wide, and 30 centimeters thick. The wall was erected in such a way as to provide strong protection for the burial chamber, which is on the south side of the shaft and is reached through an entrance in the middle of the south wall (Fig. 3).

The larger blocks were laid horizontally from east to west, and smaller blocks were arranged side by side between the slabs, from north to south (Plate 18). This method was employed to prevent the large slabs from falling, which would probably have happened if they had simply been placed on top of one another. This method of laying stones was observed for the first time in this tomb.

On entering the burial chamber, through the door at the bottom of the shaft, we found two doors, one in the east wall,

33

Figure 2

the other in the west wall. Both doors led to magazines roofed with stone blocks that were shaped in imitation of the trunks of palm trees.

The rectangular burial chamber is divided in the middle by two jambs, above which is a flat lintel (Plate 19). Behind this lintel is a second one, lower than the first and rounded, resembling the drum usually found in false doors under the lower lintel. The rounded lintel is probably a representation of a curtain to be rolled up and down.

The walls and roof of the burial chamber were well preserved. The stone slabs of the floor had been broken in places,

34

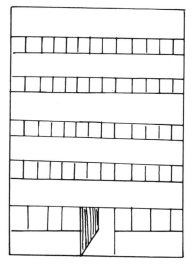

Figure 3

doubtless by robbers making soundings for possible treasure hidden beneath the floor.

In the west wall of the west magazine we found the robbers' entrance. Evidently they made this one after three unsuccessful attempts to penetrate the tomb through the south wall, from which a number of stones were removed.

In the west magazine we found a pottery lamp and water flask, probably left behind by the robbers. Both the lamp and the flask are Greco-Roman in design and fix the approximate date of the robbery.

Inside the tomb we found a large slab of white limestone with round holes bored in it, probably with crescent-shaped flint instruments. Similar stones were found in the Step Pyramid at Saqqara. We also found some stone mallets of varying sizes.

Judging from the structure of the tomb, its burial chamber, magazines, shaft, and superstructure, we are certain that it is also of the Archaic Period and was probably constructed late in the Second or early in the Third Dynasty. It is the largest stone tomb of this period so far discovered. Larger tombs have been found at Abydos and Saqqara, but they are built of mud bricks. In view of its size, this tomb must also have been built for a man of very exalted rank. The only inscription bearing a name (either of the tomb's owner or of a workman) was found on a stone in the upper part of the shaft.

The discovery of these elaborate tombs at Helwan have made it clear that not only kings but also persons of less-exalted rank were buried in tombs of stone. The burial chamber of King Udimu is paved in granite, and that of King Kha-sekhemui is built of limestone blocks. It is probable that the Helwan tombs constructed of limestone or granite were either cenotaphs of the kings or tombs of officials who lived in the reigns of those kings. The excavations at Saqqara have disclosed the impressive tombs of King Aha and King Djer.

In writing of the architectural methods of the early dynasties, Breasted wrote:

> For some four hundred years the early kings of the Second Union built their tombs of sun-dried mud brick. A group of these tombs was discovered in Upper Egypt. They are the earliest royal buildings ever found. Then, probably about 3,000 B.C., there was built in one of these brick tombs a burial

chamber of limestone blocks. This was the beginning of architecture in stone, and the direct result of the possession of tools of copper by which the stone building blocks were cut and shaped.[9]

From the discoveries at Helwan, it is evident that Egyptologists have long underestimated the genius of the people of the First and Second Dynasties and that only now can we begin to assess the true greatness of their achievements.

[9] James Henry Breasted, *Ancient Times: A History of the Early World* (2d ed., New York, Ginn & Co., 1916), 69, passage 82.

III · *Industry and Crafts*

LTHOUGH ALL THE LARGE TOMBS and most of the smaller ones had been repeatedly looted and damaged, we were able to find in them a wealth of objects created by First Dynasty craftsmen. We now possess a rich treasure of antiquities of various kinds, from accurately and beautifully made pottery jars to dishes, tables, and vessels manufactured from slate, alabaster, marble, basalt, diorite, porphyry (Frontispiece), breccia, and rock crystal. Craftsmen of the period also used copper, from which they made dishes, ewers, basins, chisels, adzes, piercers, needles, saws, knives, fishhooks, and mirrors. From flint they made knives and bracelets. From ivory they made statuettes, handles for walking sticks and fans, combs, tables, bed, and coffins.

The pottery of the First Dynasty is of astonishing excellence. Even the largest of the vessels are accurately proportioned, and the surface is as smooth as polished stone.

As mentioned earlier, in tomb 1371 H.2 we came across a large broken pottery jar dating from the reign of King Adjib (Plate 3). Since the jar was unique, being the largest recovered from the First Dynasty, we decided to restore it (Plate 20).

On some of the jars the names of kings could be discerned, and on close scrutiny the marks of the workman's hands could be seen (Plate 21). We found pottery granaries similar to those still used in rural areas today (Plate 22). Small models of these granaries were placed in the tombs with the bodies (Plate 23). Some of the models were pottery; others were made of unburned clay. We also found small pottery coffins (Plates 24 and 25).

The astonished looks on the faces of visitors to the excavations when they set eyes on such objects testify to the skill of the First Dynasty craftsmen. It is not only the accuracy of the work that amazes visitors but also the variety of forms and the artistry of the designs. Proportions are minutely observed and bear witness to advanced techniques. It is quite evident that the craftsmen approached their work with the devotion of artists, not with the reluctance of slaves laboring in *corvée*.

In tomb 24 H.5 we found a skillfully made alabaster water jug of remarkable proportions (Plate 26). The spout had been fitted with a strainer which allowed liquids to be poured from the jug drop by drop, like a medicine dropper. It is almost inconceivable that so fine a piece could have been chiseled and polished with only simple tools and primitive mallets. Moreover, it is hard to imagine how the workman bored the hole of the spout in the thin alabaster without breaking it. This achievement is further proof that the craftsmanship of this period must have been the culmination of untold generations of effort and experimentation.

Another workman left us an example of his skill in a stone bowl carved to resemble a straw basket (Plate 27). The bowl reminds one of straw baskets, called *mishanna,* still used by the country folk. The ancient Egyptian was also fond of imitating nature and often made objects resembling flowers, seeds, and plants.[1]

In our searches we found bowls and vases of slate. Two triangular bowls had been carved from blocks of slate (Plate 28). One bowl has three grooves in the sides, which are curved inward from above, as though the material out of which the bowl was carved were soft and pliable. Obviously this craftsman could control his material with the sureness of a master. The other bowl has three rounded corners and sides flowing outward. The models from which these bowls were copied were doubtless made of metal. Both resemble to some extent dishes used nowadays for fruit or candy.

The slate vases are also beautiful and well proportioned (Plate 29). Their outer surfaces are so smooth that they have a metallic luster.

In tomb 185 H.4 we found two especially lovely vases. One, carved from a black serpentine resembling ebony, has a narrow neck with a wide rim (Plate 30). The other has a similar shape and is made of rock crystal, which is, of course, even harder to cut than stone (Plate 31).

A rock-crystal bowl was also found, the largest bowl of this material yet discovered (Plate 32). It is about 13.5 centimeters tall and 22 centimeters in diameter. It is still another illustration of the skill First Dynasty artisans had achieved in working with hard materials. An especially important feature is the inscription of the name of King Smerkhet on the side of the bowl, together with the name of one Semer-

[1] Emery, *Excavations at Saqqara,* 101, Fig. 58, Plates 40A and B.

sepedou, who was probably the owner of the tomb. The bowl was no doubt a present from the king to Semer-sepedou.

In one intact magazine in tomb 423 H.9, one of the larger tombs we excavated, we found seventy bowls, vases, cups, and other items of alabaster and slate (Plates 33 and 34). When we consider that all these objects were recovered from one small magazine, we can imagine what a rich treasure the tomb originally contained. Cups with bases found in other tombs (Plate 35) are not unlike designs used in present-day glassware.

The use of copper was common in the First Dynasty. The craftsman of this period knew how to make various copper tools, such as chisels, hoes, daggers, spear- and arrowheads, saws, knives, and needles. It also occurred to him to make fishhooks of copper. He devised different sizes of hooks suitable for all kinds of angling. In tomb 741 H.5 we found ten copper hooks of varying sizes (Plate 36). It is unlikely that a modern-day fisherman's tackle box would contain a more varied assortment. To keep his hook in place, this ancient fisherman made stone weights, boring holes in them so that he could tie them to the line. Evidently his methods of catching fish were little different from those of the present-day angler. The old was the precursor of the new.

For their sewing needs the First Dynasty Egyptians made copper needles of different sizes, each size designed for a particular purpose: thin needles for sewing fine or delicate cloth, thick ones for sewing leather. The latter are strong and have wide eyes for thick thread. For heavy leatherwork, such as sandals and thongs, these ingenious people made copper piercers, to which they attached wooden handles (Plate 37).

For stonecutting they devised special tools. We found copper chisels of many different sizes and designs (Plate 38).

The modern-day Egyptian custom of washing the hands before and after meals is an inheritance from the ancient Egyptians, who for this ceremony made copper ewers and basins like those we found in tomb 129 H.6 (Plate 39). The spout of the ewer is a particularly fine example of the artisan's skill.

Large numbers of copper pans, vases, and vessels were also found. Some of these pieces were used for cooking; others served as decanters and tableware.

Flint, one of the hardest materials to cut, was deftly worked by First Dynasty craftsmen. The large, well-proportioned knives we found at Helwan are unexcelled in quality. We also found fine arm bracelets carved from flint.

As mentioned earlier, in the storeroom found intact in tomb 385 H.4 there were three large, well-made knives (Plates 40 to 42). In tomb 1226 H.9 were two flint knives of a different design (Plate 43). These knives, each about 50 centimeters long, are the largest ever discovered in Egypt.

Ivory was among the ancients' favorite materials for toilet articles and decorative objects. From it they carved boxes, dagger handles, combs, vases, walking-stick handles, mirror handles, and models of funerary boats.

While at work in tomb 116 H.4, we found, among other items, a well-executed ivory column (Plate 44). Its maker carved the piece to represent eight lotus flowers, the stalks tied together with three cords just below the flowers. The column is 21 centimeters tall. The short piece at the base, which is about 1.5 centimeters long, indicates that the column was probably part of a larger object, possibly a fan or a walking stick.

Aside from its artistry, this piece is of archaeological importance because it closely resembles the columns found at the entrance to King Zoser's Step Pyramid at Saqqara, as well as the capitals found in many temples of later dynasties. At one time it was believed that the columns in the court of the Step Pyramid were of the Doric Period, until old texts discovered on a wall of the pyramid proved beyond doubt that the columns date from the Third Dynasty. The discovery of this piece in a First Dynasty tomb indicates that such columns were built even earlier than the Third Dynasty, and probably originated in the First Dynasty.

Two ivory pieces found in tomb 8 H.8 have particularly interesting characteristics. The pieces (Plate 45) were carved to represent the front and hind hoofs and legs of a bull. The workman who could execute such pieces obviously knew the anatomy of the bull and understood the function of the muscles. Both pieces are clever representations, skillfully carved. They originally formed the bases of chair, table, or bed legs. Virtually all furniture of this period had some such ornamentation. The bases gave the furniture added height, distributed its weight evenly, and protected it from dampness.

In tomb 1 H.5 we found an ivory statuette of a hunchback. The man, obviously a servant, is kneeling with outstretched arms, humbly presenting an offering to his master (Plates 46 and 47).

Another statuette (Plate 48), also made of ivory, was found in tomb 597 H.5. It is the figure of a small boy sitting with his right elbow propped on one knee, sucking his fingers.

The palm of his left hand rests on his left knee. The artist who carved this appealing figure decorated the child's wrists with bracelets.

In another tomb was found an ivory statuette of a lion (Plate 49). Besides accurately reproducing the lion's features and limbs, the artist also captured both his spirit and his expression.

A small ivory hand (Plate 50) found in tomb 47 H.4 is an excellent piece of work. The hand, with its muscles, nails, and delicate fingers, is carefully detailed. There is no doubt that its creator also understood anatomy and musculature.

In tomb 394 H.7, a child's tomb, we found an ivory vase (Plate 51) shaped like a chrysanthemum. Each petal of the flower is delicately carved. The lid of the vase, also of ivory, represents the flower viewed from above.

Many ivory spoons were found in the tombs. One spoon (Plate 52) is large, with a long handle, while another (Plate 53) is quite small and resembles those used today in measuring minute quantities of chemicals. Other spoons have decorative handles. The handle of one, shaped like a small duck (Plate 54), has recognizable head, bill, eyes, wings, and body. The handle of another spoon is carved in the shape of the hind leg of a gazelle (Plate 55). Still another has a handle representing the emblem of the goddess Isis (Plate 56). The last spoon is of special interest because of the light it sheds on the religion of the First Dynasty Egyptians. The spoon, which is very small, was probably used to administer medicine, and the image of Isis was doubtless believed to help heal the sick.

The craftsmen of this period also turned their skills to

carving small ivory boxes, which were probably used as jewelry and ornament boxes. In tomb 627 H.6 were found the remains of a cylindrical ivory box (Plate 57). It is 12 centimeters in diameter; its height could not be determined. It is made of long, narrow ivory splints, arranged in a crisscross design.

In tomb 61 H.10 we found an inlaid-ivory box (Plates 58 and 59). It is 22 centimeters long, 11.5 centimeters wide, and 6.5 centimeters high. The lid is made of the same material.

In tomb 115 H.10 we found pieces of ivory inlay from the sides and lid of a box. Restored, the box measures 26 centimeters long, 14.7 centimeters wide, and 15 centimeters high (Plates 60 and 61). The box lid is particularly attractive. In each corner, inside the border, is an inlaid-ivory leaf. In the center are eight flowers.

Artisans of the period also used shells for inlay work. In tomb 636 H.4 we found a box containing remains of the skeleton of a very small child (Plate 62). The box, which was in extremely poor condition, was also restored (Plate 63).

It was the custom of the ancient Egyptians to bury their pets either with their owners or in separate graves nearby. Not far from one tomb we found a grave containing a small wooden box (Plate 64). After treating the box with a preservative, we were able to remove it from the grave. The box contained the bones of a bird, probably a hawk (Plate 65).

THE OBJECTS DESCRIBED in the foregoing pages comprise but a small portion of the Helwan discoveries. They are an important addition to our store of knowledge about the First

Dynasty. Not only do they reveal an amazing artistry, but they offer invaluable guidance in our efforts to illuminate that remote and shadowy era.

IV · *Dress and Customs*

THE CLOTHES WORN by First Dynasty Egyptians were generally made of linen. In the Helwan tombs we found many kinds of linen, indicating a wide variety in clothing.

In tomb 1 H.9 we found pottery objects resembling the wooden shuttles used today in hand looms. Other pieces resemble the pegs used in adjusting looms (Plate 66). Much of the cloth we found is even and straight, as well woven as the best modern machine-loomed material. The thread is so fine that one can hardly believe it was spun with a simple spindle. Some pieces of cloth are extremely thin and smooth (Plate 67), while others are heavy and coarse (Plate 68). No doubt the lighter cloth was intended for summer use while the heavier cloth was used in winter.

It is also noteworthy that in tomb 36 H.5 we found the remains of a man wrapped in a woolen cloth. Until this discovery the use of wool in the First Dynasty was unknown to Egyptologists. On many of the Second Dynasty stelae, or funerary tablets, found in the tombs are mentioned several kinds of cloth of different colors—red, white, green, and blue.

The robes worn in these periods were long, reaching to

Figure 4

the feet. Some had sleeves, while others were sleeveless and were tied over one shoulder with ribbons—in most cases the left shoulder (Fig. 4 and Plate 69). Some of the robes were draped low across the back and front and secured with straps. Members of the upper classes wore sandals made of leather or straw. Evidently the king's sandal bearer held a high position in court; stelae show him standing directly behind the king.

From carvings found on tomb stelae we can assume that hair styling was an important aspect of grooming. Men's hair was evidently worn to the nape of the neck and shaped to cover the ears or brushed behind the ears (Fig. 5A to D). Occasionally the hair was allowed to fall naturally to the shoulders (Fig. 5E). One stela pictures a more complicated style (Fig. 5F), plaits of hair to which a false fringe is attached. The sophistication and care in styling indicate that the art of hairdressing had been practiced for some time.

Women's hair was worn much longer and was sometimes plaited (Fig. 6A to C). Occasionally strands of hair were combed across the shoulders and allowed to fall loosely across the breasts, in much the same style as that of the modern-day girl (Fig. 6D to F). One stela shows a lady, seated on a caned chair, her hair nicely dressed, with even-lengthed tresses falling down her back and over her shoulders (Fig. 7 and Plate 70).

To dress their hair, the Egyptians used combs of ivory, wood, and other materials. Some were curved to fit the head and to hold a wig in place or to hold the hair behind the ears. Some had long teeth, and others had short teeth. In tomb 621 H.5 we found a short-toothed ivory comb with a case

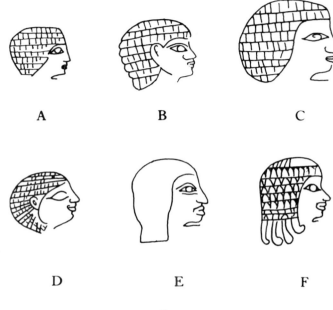

A   B   C

D   E   F

Figure 5

made of straw. In tomb 17 H.8 was a symbolic comb made of polished slate (Plate 72). The comb is evidently an invention of remote antiquity. Many have been found in prehistoric sites.

After the lady of the First Dynasty had completed the task of dressing her hair, she applied a reddish powder to her cheeks. Then she darkened her eyelids with kohl, which she applied with an ivory kohl stick. In a jar in tomb 826 H.2 we found samples of three kinds of kohl. Laboratory analysis showed the samples to consist of galena, malachite, and hematite. Galena, lead sulphide, was used by the ancient Egyptians to make black kohl. Malachite, a green basic copper carbonate, was used to make green kohl. Hematite, an ore of iron, was used in making brown kohl, which was not commonly used in ancient times. These substances were ground to a powder and mixed with an adhesive, which was probably a gum solution. The kohl samples found at Helwan are the oldest so far discovered. It is unusual to find three samples in the same jar.

In tomb 1448 H.2 we found a jar containing a gray material that proved to be composed of silica, lead sulphide, iron and aluminum oxide, calcium sulphate, magnesium sulphate, sodium chloride, and water. This material was undoubtedly gray kohl, perhaps the earliest sample of kohl of that color recovered from ancient times.

The selection of well-formed ivory kohl sticks we found at the site (Plate 73) is strong evidence that the women of that remote period shared with their modern sisters a love of elegant toilet articles.

Numerous vases were found containing several kinds of

Figure 6

perfumes and ointments. On analysis the ointments were found to be composed mainly of fatty materials (primarily from animals) mixed with red iron oxide and ground limestone (calcium carbonate). Mixed with these substances, no doubt, were other oils, which have evaporated without trace. The ointments were used to smooth the face and give it a rosy color. In applying them, the women of ancient Egypt, like her counterpart today, used a mirror like the wooden-handled one made of copper found at Helwan (Plate 74).

The colors used in these cosmetics were usually ground on slate palettes. One palette we found is rectangular in shape (Plate 75). The sides are decorated with upraised arms in the form of the ka. At the top are three hieroglyphs denoting prosperity, life, and happiness. The palette in effect asks the god to bestow on its owner a prosperous and happy life. Another slate palette is carved to represent a fish (Plate 76). The eyes are formed from pieces of shell.

Jewelry was worn by both men and women. At the Helwan site we found many necklaces, some of carnelian, hematite, and alabaster beads, others of green, blue, and white faïence beads. The beads vary from small, round ones to long, cylindrical ones. Some necklaces are made of only one type and color of beads, while others are of different shapes and colors—for example, alternating beads of red carnelian and alabaster. Other necklaces are white, red, green, and blue (Plate 77). The ancient Egyptian lady evidently acquired a large selection of jewelry. In one tomb alone we discovered seven necklaces and nine bracelets (Plate 78).

A large pectoral, made of faïence beads, was discovered in one of the First Dynasty tombs (Plate 79). Until this dis-

Figure 7

covery Egyptologists had believed that pectorals were first made in the Fourth Dynasty. Pectorals were made not only of faïence but also of semiprecious stones, such as carnelian, amethyst, and lapis lazuli.

In the tombs we also found pendants, some carved in the forms of animals and reptiles, others representing the falcon in the solar bark of the god Ra. The ancient jewelers also carved realistic replicas of hippopotamuses and of flies and other insects.

In tomb 440 H.5 were found four green faïence necklaces of flat, round beads. With the necklaces was a broken wheel of green faïence (Plates 80 and 81). The wheel was probably designed to be worn as a pendant. In the wheel are eight spokes (Plate 81). Seven spokes are similar, while the eighth is of a different design (Fig. 8A). While I was studying the wheel-like object, it occurred to me that if the circle was disregarded and the wheel turned with the dissimilar spoke pointing downward (Fig. 8B), the piece resembled the trunk and crown of a palm tree (Fig. 8C and D).[1]

The bracelets found at Helwan are made of faïence, ivory, mother-of-pearl, and slate (Plates 82 and 83). Those made of slate and ivory are of varying widths. The wide bracelets were worn on the upper arm by men, women, and children. In the tombs we found specimens on the remains of arms of both sexes (Plate 84).

Oval-shaped dolomite objects, with holes bored at each

---

[1] The palm tree was a representation of the goddess Seshat. See C. A. Wainwright, "Seshat and the Pharaoh," *The Journal of Egyptian Archaeology,* Vol. 26 (London, 1942). See also Vivi Tackholm and Mohamed Drar, *Bulletin of Science,* No. 38, 210–14.

end, were found beside the wristbones of the dead (Plate 85). These objects must also have been worn as bracelets, tied around the wrists. They may well have been the First Dynasty version of modern-day identification bracelets.

THE MANNER IN WHICH a society provides for its food and the varieties of foods it utilizes are significant keys to its civilization and standards of living. From the tombs excavated at Helwan, as well as from the excavation projects at Saqqara, we have learned much about the foods and eating habits of First and Second Dynasty Egyptians. It was a religious custom to store quantities of food in the tomb magazines so that the dead would have nourishment in the other world. From the types of storage jars we found there, and even from actual remains of food, as well as from scenes on tomb walls and stelae, we were able to reconstruct the diet of the people.

They were accustomed to eating many different kinds of meat, such as mutton, goat, beef, and gazelle. They ate game birds, such as geese, ducks, quails, and pigeons. They were also extremely fond of fish. Vegetables and fruits were important elements of their diet. They ate lentils, beans, radishes, onions, and garlic. Fruits included figs, grapes, dates, raisins, pomegranates, and melons. Their bread was made from different kinds of grain, including wheat flour. They baked the loaves in round, triangular, and conical shapes. They also made cakes and pies. They drank milk from cows, goats, and sheep, and also made cheese and butter. They made wine from grapes, beer from barley, and arrack from dates.

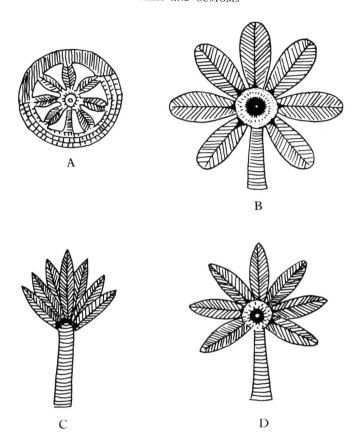

A

B

C

D

Figure 8

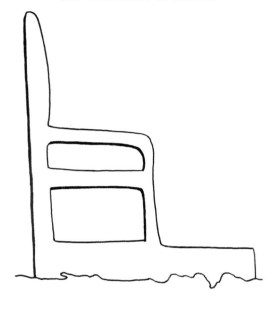

Figure 9

The typical meal of the well-to-do Egyptian consisted of several courses. In Saqqara, beside the coffin of a highly placed man of the Second Dynasty, we found a complete meal, together with tableware of alabaster, marble, and slate. The foods, which had been placed in pottery serving dishes in a symbolic effort to keep them hot, were in a good state of preservation, and we were able to identify among them quail, fish, beef, pigeon stuffed with rice, and different kinds of vegetables. In one of the dishes were two pieces of kidney. There were also round and triangular cakes.

Three dishes could not be identified. The meal thus consisted of about twelve courses.

Near the dishes were pottery jars which had probably contained wine, beer, or arrack. Next to the jars were smaller earthenware jars still sealed with clay stoppers. On them were written in black ink the names of the fruits preserved in them.

Stelae reveal that First Dynasty Egyptians ate their meals seated on chairs at tables. The chairs were of different kinds and designs, indicating that furniture makers had an inventive spirit and liked variations in style. Some chairs were comfortable ones with arms and high backs (Fig. 9) and were similar in design to modern chairs. Another chair pictured on a stela has a low back and is evidently covered with a protective cloth (Fig. 10). A third, with huge legs, appears to have straw padding (Fig. 11). A fourth is cushioned and

Figure 10

Figure 11

Figure 12   Figure 13

has legs carved in imitation of bulls' legs and hoofs (Fig. 12). The fifth chair has similarly carved legs and a cushion, which is evidently tied to the legs, as indicated by the vertical lines on the sides (Fig. 13).

Though we did not find any beds in the excavations at Helwan, we know that First Dynasty Egyptians used them. Numerous specimens from that period have been found at Saqqara.[2]

THE FIRST DYNASTY EGYPTIAN was a farsighted person. When he tilled the soil, he planted crops that would provide food for himself and for his animals, as well as the materials he needed to make clothing. He grew wheat, barley, and lentils, and he sowed the flax from which he made his cloth (Plates 67 and 68).

When he gathered his harvest, he stored what he would

[2] Emery and Saad, *The Tomb of Hor-Aha*, 63–64.

62

need to sustain him until the next crop. He invented granaries in which to store wheat, a practice still followed in Egypt and other agricultural countries. At Helwan we discovered granaries used for storing crops and seed (Plate 22). In a storeroom in tomb 1502 H.2 we came across four pottery granaries containing wheat and barley grain and lentil seeds (Plate 86).

Beside another tomb we discovered a rectangular hole containing the remains of five large granaries made of mud bricks (Plate 87). What was left of the granaries indicates that they were wider at the base than at the top and that they were at least 3 meters tall.[3]

Hunting game was a common pursuit in the forests and on the desert bordering the fertile valley. We found several ibex horns in the excavations. Beside one of the bigger tombs we found a large pair of horns that had been broken and mended, indicating that they were highly valued (Plate 88). It is likely that they decorated a wall in the house of the tomb's owner and were buried with him along with other funerary objects. There is no way to determine whether the man was a professional hunter or merely hunted for sport. The latter possibility seems the more likely, since the size of the tomb indicates that he was a man of high rank.

Bows and arrows and spears were the weapons used in hunting. We found a large number of arrowheads, some made of flint, others of ivory. These weapons were also used in war, as were swords and daggers, which had copper blades and wooden or ivory handles.

[3] Zaki Y. Saad, *The Royal Excavations at Helwan* (Cairo, 1945–47), 20, Plates XVIII*b*, XIX*a*, *b*.

The presence of many varieties and sizes of fishhooks and line weights, described earlier, indicates that fishing was also popular both as a profession and as a sport.

The ancient Egyptian, particularly one who belonged to the upper class, evidently had plenty of leisure time. To entertain family and friends he invented several indoor games and amusements. Some of the games were found in the Helwan tombs. One, evidently a game something like draughts, was discovered intact. It consists of seven conical pieces and seven hemispherical ones, carved from alabaster, together with sixty rounds of beads of different shapes, colors, and materials (Plate 89). We had found similar beads in other tombs and had thought that they were placed in the tombs to be used in making necklaces in the other world. But their occurrence with this game suggests that they must have been used for scoring or betting, much as poker chips are used today. We do not know exactly how the game was played. Ivory game pieces of varying shapes were also found in other tombs. These were probably used in a game similar to chess (Plate 90). Such games, obviously of some complexity, are evidence that these people had achieved an advanced stage of intellectual development.

As for outdoor games, here is no doubt that First Dynasty Egyptians played the same ones as those depicted on the walls of tombs built in later periods. We found no traces of them at Helwan, no doubt simply because it did not occur to the people to picture them on the tomb walls. They may have recorded the games on papyrus rolls which have since disappeared.

V · *Writing*

WRITING HAD BEEN INVENTED in Egypt long before the First Dynasty. Evidence of this fact is the degree of perfection shown in inscriptions carved during the period. A beginner in penmanship must write slowly, forming his letters one at a time, and even then the result is far from perfect. At Helwan we found earthenware jars bearing names written in a running script that clearly reveals mastery of writing skills. Elsewhere the names of kings are inscribed in accurate, well-formed characters that could have been carved only by someone used to the art of writing. On one alabaster fragment we found the name of King Aha incised in a beautiful hand (Plate 91). Perched on top of the *serekh* is a well-carved falcon holding a spear in its claws.

On a fragment of slate was found the name of King Qaa, the last king of the First Dynasty, also well incised, together with a falcon perched on top of the *serekh*. Here again the king's name is so well written that it suggests a writing tradition of long duration (Plate 92).

In tomb 728 H.5 we found ivory fragments with hiero-

Figure 14

glyphic inscriptions. The pieces were restored and revealed the name of Queen Neit-hetep, the wife of King Aha. Below the inscriptions is carved the face of the queen (Fig. 14 and Plate 93). Even though the lower part of the fragment could not be found, we were nevertheless fortunate in this discovery: it is the first representation we have of the face of Queen Neit-hetep, who ruled Lower Egypt until she was married to King Aha and united Upper and Lower Egypt under one ruling family.[1]

This marriage is said to have been the first political marriage in history. Obviously the union of the two kingdoms

[1] Drioton and Vandier, *Les Peuples de l'orient Mediterranéan: II. Égypte,* 137, 139.

was a peaceful one and was accomplished with the consent of the people. Soon after the marriage took place, King Aha felt safe in leaving the kingdom to embark on his Nubian and Libyan conquests.[2] From the time of the marriage inscriptions began to show the crowns of both kingdoms appearing together as a double crown.

The tomb of King Aha was discovered in the cemetery at Saqqara.[3] This discovery confirms the theory that Aha took up residence in the new capital of Memphis (the "White Wall"). It is not conceivable that if the king had lived in This, the old capital near Abydos, he would have been buried at Saqqara. It would not have been possible to transport his body so great a distance for burial, since the art of embalming had not yet been discovered.

It was evidently the custom of First Dynasty Egyptians to write the name of the tomb's owner and that of the contemporary king on the stoppers of pottery jars and other objects that were to be placed in the tombs. One such stopper was found in a Helwan tomb. The inscription, which is partly obliterated, is probably the name of King Djer (Plate 94).

The stoppers were usually made of clay mixed with straw or palm fibers. Before the stoppers dried, a cylindrical seal bearing both names was rolled across them, leaving the impression on the sides. On one soapstone seal (Plate 95), described on page 27, is the representation of King Aha. Another seal (Plate 96), made of hematite, is notable for the clarity and accuracy of its carvings.

[2] *Ibid.,* 138.
[3] Emery and Saad, *The Tomb of Hor-Aha.*

The contents of the vases and the name of the tomb's owner were also inscribed on ivory tablets, which served as labels. A picture of the vase itself was sometimes drawn on the tablet. In tomb 635 H.9 we found three such tablets, on which appear the name of the owner, a description of the contents of the vase, and a picture of the vase (Plate 97). In the upper right corner of each tablet one can discern a hole through which a cord was strung to tie the tablet to the neck of the vase.

We found several inkholders of the period. Most of them were made of slate, an impervious stone. One rectangular slate inkholder had two circular wells to hold black and red ink, the colors used in the period (Plate 98). In tomb 270 H.5 was another rectangular inkholder, divided into two compartments with a lid fitting into a groove around them (Plates 99 and 100). This inkholder was found beside the head of the dead man (Plate 101), indicating that he was probably a scribe.

Unfortunately, we could not find any specimens of the pens used by First Dynasty writers. Judging from the nature of the inscriptions, we believe that they probably used pens made from reeds.

VI · *Transportation*

$\mathbf{F}$IRST AND SECOND DYNASTY EGYPTIANS had little choice in their means of transportation: they could travel on foot, by donkey, or by boat. The peasants generally walked. When traveling some distance by land, the king and members of the court rode donkeys. Evidently the Egyptians were extremely fond of their donkeys and valued them highly. They often had them buried in special tombs close to their own. This little beast of burden is still an important means of transportation in the hinterlands of Egypt and is still regarded with affection.

To travel up and down the Nile the ancient Egyptians used various types of boats. Some were constructed of small pieces of wood joined together. Others were constructed of papyrus stems tied together in bundles and sealed to prevent leakage. The papyrus boat was generally used in the marshes and shallows, since the frailty of the craft made it unreliable in deep or rapid water. Both types of boats continued in use for many centuries.

For transporting building stones and other supplies on the river, the Egyptians constructed wooden floats and rafts. No indication of their size has yet been discovered, but to judge from the size of the blocks of stone transported on them, they must have been quite large.

Early in the excavation work at Helwan we came across the model of a boat carved from ivory (Plate 102). The model was not intact; the stern of the vessel was missing. Since the tomb in which it was found had not been robbed, we could only conclude that the model was already broken when it was placed in the tomb.[1] Another boat model, carved from yellow limestone (Plate 103), and a third, made of pottery (Plate 104), were found later. The sterns of these boats were also missing. So far we have not been able to determine any reason, secular or religious, for the fact that all the models were broken. All of them were found in tombs of modest dimensions.

Even more significant were our discoveries of the remains of actual wooden boats buried in the ground near many of the tombs. The first boat was found south of tomb 1051 H.2. It is one of the larger specimens we recovered, though it is smaller than those found at the royal tombs at Saqqara. A second boat was found west of tomb 649 H.5 (Plate 105), a third north of tomb 680 H.5, and a fourth north of tomb 762 H.5.

In a later season we discovered three boats buried north of three medium-sized tombs (Plates 106 to 108), and the following season we found seven more, all but one buried north of their respective tombs. In all we found the remains of nineteen boats. The mounds covering the boats resembled the backs of surfacing whales, tapering to a point at each end.

[1] Saad, *The Royal Excavations at Saqqara and Helwan.*

Obviously boats were owned by members of the upper classes, and not merely by the royal family. From the size of the ones we found at Helwan we can assume that even larger vessels were used on the Nile as pleasure craft and also for long-distance travel. We have ample evidence pointing to the use of oars to move these vessels, but it is not known for certain whether sails were common in the First and Second Dynasties. Future discoveries may provide further information on this point.

There has been much conjecture about the purpose of the boats buried near the tombs at Helwan. They may have been intended to provide transport in the other world, or they may have served as symbols of death and passage to the other world. More evidence must be provided by spade and trowel before we can be certain about the purpose of these craft. It seems obvious that they had some religious significance, about which more will be said in Chapter VII.

There is no question that the ease of travel—and therefore of communication and trade—provided by the great river Nile is one of the most important reasons for the advanced civilization achieved by this remarkable people.

VII · *Religion*

$\mathbf{L}$IKE OTHER GREAT RELIGIONS, the religion of the ancient Egyptians evolved gradually, paralleling the development of their culture, arts, and science. However, the discoveries made in the Helwan excavations indicate that the religion of the Archaic Period was much more advanced than Egyptologists had hitherto believed. In the Helwan tombs we found symbols of deities once believed to have evolved in later periods. Evidently these ancient peoples had arrived at an advanced and complex religion.

Among other pieces we found ivory symbols of the god Osiris (Plate 109). These pieces, symbols of Osiris as a fertility god, are shaped like cypress trees, with straight trunks and branches tied together in layers.

Equally interesting was the discovery of the symbol of the goddess Isis on an ivory spoon handle (Plate 110, left). Another ivory piece, probably part of the lid of a small coffer, was found bearing two well-executed symbols of Isis and below them the hieroglyphic sign *hetep,* meaning "peace" (Plate 110, right).

From the tombs we recovered many pieces representing

the falcon, which was the emblem of the god Horus, the son of Osiris and Isis (Plate 111A to D). Another piece, in the form of a vulture, represents the goddess Nekhbet, who was worshipped in the nome of Nekhen (Plate 111E).

We came across numerous articles made of faïence and alabaster representing the emblems of the fertility god Min (Plate 112). Some of the Min pieces have holes in the center, while some of the Horus symbols have holes in the lower part, below the legs. At first we believed that these emblems had been placed separately on some sort of stand, like a totem pole, but later we found a copper emblem representing Horus crouching on the emblem of Min (Plate 113). We then concluded that at one time the faïence emblems of Min must have been surmounted by the emblems of Horus and that the pieces were later broken apart. The significance of these discoveries lies in the fact that they are the earliest known pieces showing the union of two gods who, according to legend, had long engaged in warfare that was finally ended by the decisive victory of Horus.

The discovery of such a large number of emblems proves beyond doubt that the Egyptians worshiped these gods and goddesses at least as early as the First Dynasty, and probably even earlier.

Until the discovery of the large First Dynasty tombs at Saqqara, the practice of placing funerary barks with the bodies of the dead was believed to have begun in the Fourth Dynasty and to have been limited to members of the royal family. When a brick grave containing a wooden bark was discovered north of King Aha's tomb at Saqqara,[1] and an-

[1] Emery and Saad, *The Tomb of Hor-Aha*, 8–9, Plate 3.

other north of Hemaka's tomb,[2] Egyptologists realized that the practice had begun much earlier.

As mentioned in Chapter VI, in the excavations at Helwan we discovered the remains of nineteen funerary barks,[3] as well as models of such boats. From this discovery we concluded that the custom of burying boats near the dead was followed not only for royalty but also for members of the upper classes, and even for commoners. Moreover, it seems clear that both kings and commoners of the First and Second Dynasties worshiped the god Ra, for one of the purposes of the barks was doubtless to transport the owners when they joined the procession of the sun god around the earth. The poor, who could not afford real boats, had to content themselves with models.

The false doors and stelae we found in the Helwan tombs opened exciting avenues of conjecture. The stelae forming the upper part of the false doors were generally made of white limestone and, rarely, of wood. On the typical stela is carved the figure of the man buried in the tomb, seated in a chair, his name and title carved above his head. Before him is a table covered with food, and in the space behind the table are offerings of clothing, food, and drink.

In tombs excavated in other cemeteries the false door was invariably placed in the west wall of the superstructure so that the carving of the dead man faced the east. Behind the door was a shaft that led down to the burial chamber. It was

[2] Hemaka was a noble who lived during the reign of Udimu and served as chancellor to the king. He bore the title "Ruling in the King's Heart." His tomb at Saqqara was discovered and excavated in 1936. (See Emery and Saad, *The Tomb of Hemaka.*)

[3] Saad, *The Royal Excavations at Saqqara and Helwan,* 111, Plate LIXa.

believed that the function of the false door was to allow the soul of the dead man to pass through it to eat food from the offering table and then return to the burial chamber. In Second Dynasty tombs at the Helwan cemetery we discovered what we believe was the original purpose of the false door.

In these tombs we were astonished to find the doors placed in the southwest section of the ceilings of the burial chambers. In each tomb the stela was fixed at the end of a hole in the ground (which was later filled with debris), positioned to face the body inside the chamber. Our conclusion was that Egyptians of the Second Dynasty believed that the soul of the dead departed to heaven at the moment of death and that later, when the soul descended to its grave, it could pass through the hole and identify its original body from the portrait on the stela.

Thus it appears that only later did the Egyptians come to believe that the soul remained in the tomb with the body, at which time the original significance of the false door was changed and the door came to serve as a symbolic means of passage to and from the burial chamber.

I must make it clear that this theory has by no means been universally accepted. But the position of the stelae in the Second Dynasty tombs at Helwan seems to allow no other explanation.

In each of the First Dynasty tombs at Saqqara there are two chapels in the mastaba, both facing eastward. One of the chapels is larger than the other. The larger chapel is south of the east wall of the superstructure, while the smaller one is north of the east wall. When we excavated the necropolis at Helwan, we found to our surprise that in all the First Dynasty tombs the chapels were in the west wall of the mastaba, facing west (Plate 10). Thus the Helwan chapels face the setting, not the rising sun.

How can we explain this curious difference in the architectural features of two cemeteries dating from the same period? The answer to this question may lie in the positions of the cemeteries in relation to the Nile. Among other gods, the ancient Egyptians worshiped the Nile deity, Hapi. It seems probable that in his honor they built the chapels in both cemeteries to face the river and the fertile valley that sustained and nurtured them.

This theory, too, is a tentative one. Despite the enormous amount of information archaeologists have accumulated about the ancient Egyptians, much of their religion remains clothed in mystery, and we are still compelled to use deductive methods in our efforts to decipher its phenomena.

VIII · *Burial*

DURING THE FIRST AND SECOND DYNASTIES the dead were buried with the bodies lying in the position of the human fetus before birth. Immediately after death, before the limbs hardened, the knees were drawn up in front of the chest with the feet close to the pelvis. The hands were placed in front of the face (Plate 114). Then the body was placed in the tomb lying on one side, usually the left, with the head either to the north or to the south. The body was not generally placed directly on the floor, but was usually wrapped in cloth and placed in a coffin made of clay, pottery, wood, or plant stems (Plates 24, 25, and 115).

The ancient Egyptian looked upon the earth as a second mother. He believed that, by being buried in this position, at resurrection he would emerge from Mother Earth as he had emerged from the womb of his natural mother.

As described in Chapter II, the tombs of the poor were simply rectangular or oval graves with no superstructure. Some of the graves had funerary objects (Plates 101 and 114); others did not (Plate 116). The more elaborate tombs had one storeroom either on the north or on the south (Plate 117), while others contained two storerooms, one on the north and another on the south. In some tombs as many as four storerooms were found (Plate 118).

Most tombs were intended for one body. Only very rarely did we find a tomb containing more than one skeleton (Plate 119). In cases where two or three bodies were placed in the same tomb, we must assume that all the people buried there died at the same time, for tombs were roofed immediately after the bodies were placed in them, not to be reopened.

In a Second Dynasty tomb containing two burial chambers, we found skeletons of five bodies in one chamber and three in the other (Fig. 15). When the five skeletons in the first chamber were examined, they were found to be those of an adult male, an adult female, and three children. The skeletons in the second burial chamber were those of an adult male, an adult female, and a child. Both groups were probably families, all of whose members died at the same time.

As mentioned earlier, animals were often buried near their owners' tombs. Donkeys were sometimes buried in special tombs (Plate 120). In tomb 53 H.3 we found the skeleton of three large donkeys. Pets were sometimes buried in their masters' tombs. In one tomb we found a dog wrapped in a cloth and placed in a coffin. The dog was even provided with food for its life in the other world (Plate 121). We also discovered some tombs containing skeletons of birds in wooden or pottery coffins (Plates 64 and 65).

The art of embalming had not yet been discovered, but owing to the dryness of the site many of the skeletons we

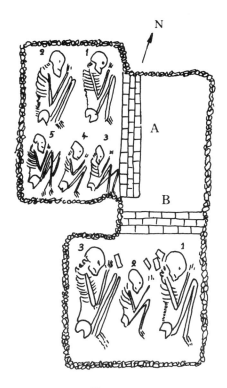

Figure 15

found were reasonably well preserved. On some of the skulls even the skin and hair remained (Plates 122 and 123).

When the tombs at Helwan were first discovered, it was thought that they had belonged to members of the lower classes. As the work advanced and many large-sized tombs were excavated, it became evident that many of the tombs had belonged to high officials of the royal courts.

On various objects we found the names of the following First Dynasty kings: Narmer, Aha, Djer, Udimu, Adjib, Smerkhet, and Qaa. Only one name, that of King Djet, is missing. We found one royal name of the Second Dynasty, King Neterimu. We also found the following names, classified according to rank:

Princes: Hequet-khenemet, Sat-sat

Princesses: Dohen-rod, Nefer, Upe, Nefer-set, Gefa, Sakhou, Kakhet

Gentlemen: Nefer-meri-ka, Khou-itef, Nebo, Irni, Nisu-hedjet, Iosen-get, Sisi

Ladies: Nisu-heket, Menkhet-ka, Douat-neit, Heken, Nisi-neit (twice), Bat, Nefer-Sioof

From their titles we can judge that the Helwan necropolis was the cemetery of members of the upper classes. The small tombs surrounding the larger ones are doubtless those of their servants.

IX · *Conclusion*

THIS BOOK IS BUT A BRIEF REPORT on the discoveries at Helwan. After studying our finds, those of us who participated in the project reached a number of conclusions, the most important of which are summarized below.

First Dynasty Egyptians used stone in constructing their tombs, not merely mud bricks. Since the tombs were doubtless imitations of their earthly homes, these homes were probably also built of stone. The durable and skillful construction of the tombs indicate advanced architectural abilities, no doubt the result of generations of experiment.

Many Egyptologists hold the view that the ancient Egyptians were primarily interested in building and furnishing their tombs and had little interest in their earthly homes. They also contend that the houses of the ancients were very small and lacking in architectural sophistication. To me, both theories seem to have little merit. The original houses constructed by these people were destroyed during repeated invasions of Egypt by foreign powers, and it is certain that foreign rulers did not permit them to build new ones of the size and style of their ancestors' homes.

The jars, tableware, and decorative objects recovered from the Helwan tombs testify to the skill in arts and crafts the people had achieved by the First Dynasty, as well as their obvious appreciation of works of art.

The life of the upper classes of the First Dynasty was evidently an easy one, in which there was abundant food and ample leisure time for hobbies and intellectual pursuits. The art of writing was familiar one and had doubtless been handed down from a time preceding the union of Upper and Lower Egypt.

First and Second Dynasty Egyptians had advanced religious beliefs. In their devotion to their duties they developed a spiritual quality that could not but be an impelling force in the advancement of their arts and culture.

In short, the Helwan excavations revealed the people of the Archaic Period to be in every way fitting precursors of the Pharaohs of the splendid ages to come. When they built their white-walled tombs, they built not only for the dead but also for the ages.

Plates

Plate I   Aerial photograph of a portion of the Helwan
excavations

Plate 2 Magazines in tomb 1371 H.2 (the measuring stick is marked off in 10-centimeter sections)

Plate 3   Limestone-paved burial chamber in tomb 1371 H.2
with large pottery jar *in situ*

Plate 4   Pottery-jar stopper bearing the name of King Adjib

Plate 5   Remains of the mastaba of tomb 1374 H.2

Plate 6   Mud-brick staircase in tomb 1374 H.2

Plate 7   Staircase, door, and magazines of tomb 785 H.5

Plate 8   Remains of four upper magazines in tomb 785 H.5

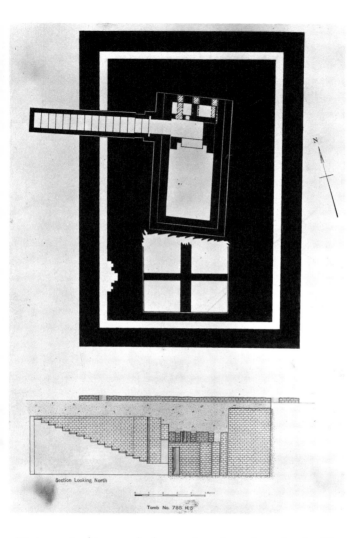

Section Looking North

Tomb No. 785 H.5

Plate 9 Architectural plan and section of tomb 785 H.5

Plate 10 Chapel west of tomb 785 H.5, with offering jars *in situ*

Plate 11   Slabs of limestone forming the roof of tomb
423 H.9

Plate 12   Mastaba of tomb 423 H.9

Plate 13   Interior of the mastaba of tomb 423 H.9

Plate 14　Staircase and portcullises of tomb 1 H.3

Plate 15   Stone steps, portcullises, and walls of tomb 40 H.3

Plate 16   Stone courses and lintel in tomb 1390 H.2

Plate 17   Limestone slabs in tomb 385 H.4

Plate 18   Rectangular shaft in the mastaba of tomb 287 H.6

Plate 19   Burial chamber and drum lintel in tomb 287 H.6

Plate 21   Pottery jars bearing the names of kings

Plate 20   Restored pottery jar from tomb 1371 H.2

Plate 22 Large pottery granaries found in tombs 1371 H.2

Plate 23 Models of granaries made of pottery and clay

Plate 24   Pottery coffin *in situ* in tomb 883 H.2

Plate 25   Pottery coffin found in tomb 268 H.6

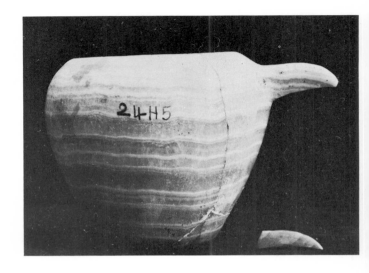

Plate 26   Alabaster jug and strainer found in tomb 24 H.5

Plate 27   Stone bowl carved in imitation of a straw basket

Plate 28 Two bowls carved from slate found in tomb
683 H.5

Plate 29   Vases carved from slate

Plate 30   Serpentine vase found
in tomb 185 H.4

Plate 31   Rock-crystal vase found
in tomb 185 H.4

Plate 32 Rock-crystal bowl bearing the names of King Smerkhet and Semer-sepedou

118

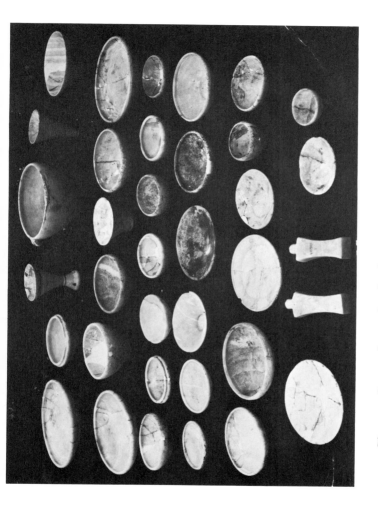

Plate 33   Group of vases, bowls, plates, and cups found in tomb 423 H.9

Plate 34   Group of plates and bowls found in tomb 423 H.9

Plate 35 Cups with bases

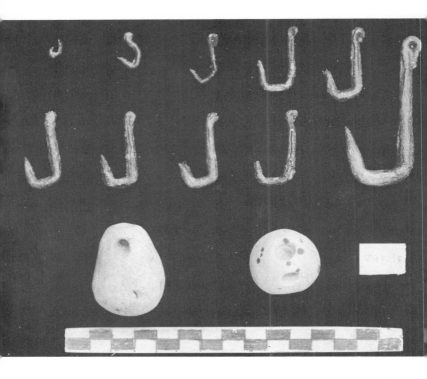

Plate 36   Copper fishhooks and stone weights found in
tomb 741 H.5

Plate 37 Copper sewing needles and wooden-handled
piercer

Plate 38   Selection of copper chisels

Plate 39 Copper ewer and basin found in tomb 129 H.6

Plate 40   Large flint knife found in a magazine of
tomb 385 H.4

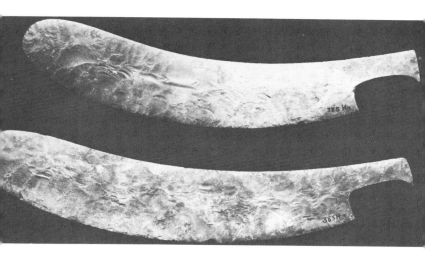

Plate 41   Two large flint knives found in a magazine of
tomb 385 H.4

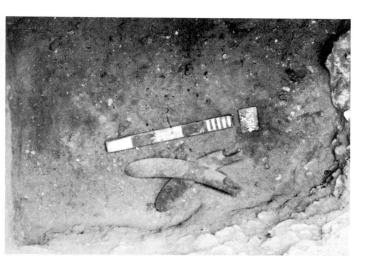

Plate 42   Flint knives shown in Plate 41 *in situ* at the bottom of the magazine in tomb 385 H.4

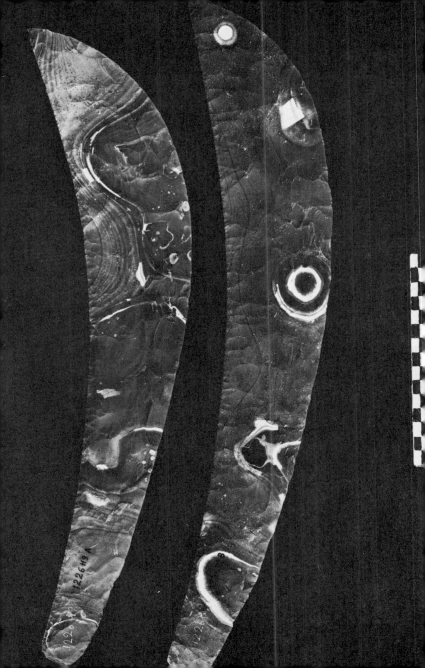

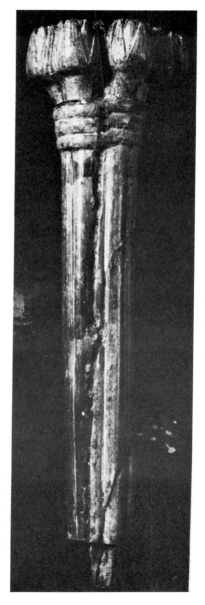

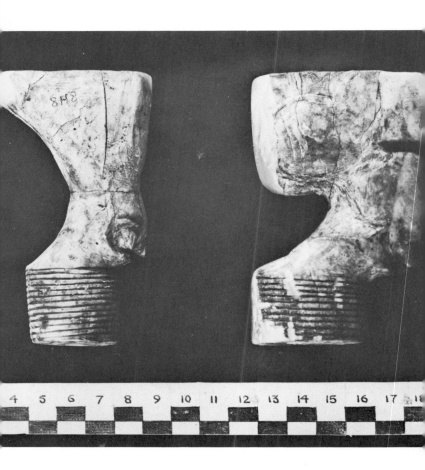

Plate 45 Ivory furniture bases carved in the shape of a
bull's hoofs, found in tomb 8 H.8

130

Plate 46 Ivory statuette of a kneeling man found in tomb 1 H.5

Plate 47 Profile of statuette shown in Plate 46

Plate 48   Ivory carving of a small boy

Plate 49   Ivory carving of a lion

Plate 50   Ivory hand found in tomb 47 H.4

Plate 51 Ivory vase and lid carved in the shape of a
chrysanthemum

Plate 53
Small ivory spoon
found in tomb 104 H.4

Plate 52   Large ivory spoon

136

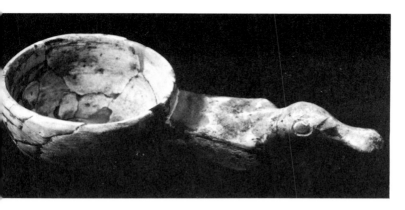

Plate 54 Ivory spoon with the handle carved in a form of
a duck

Plate 55 Ivory spoon with the handle carved in the form
of a gazelle's leg

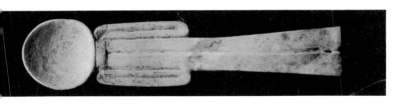

Plate 56 Ivory spoon with the handle carved in the form
of the symbol of Isis

Plate 57 Cylindrical box made of narrow ivory splints

61 H.10

Plate 58   Inlaid-ivory box found in tomb 61 H.10

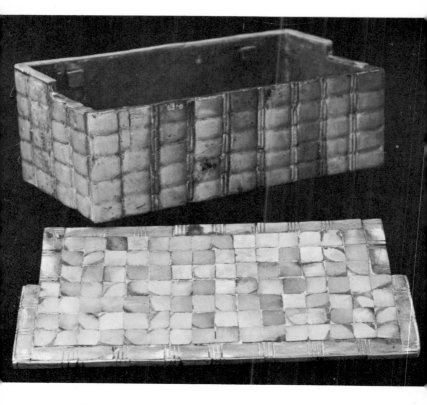

Plate 59   Ivory box shown in Plate 58 with the lid removed

Plate 60   Inlaid-ivory box found in tomb 115 H.10 and
restored

Plate 61   Restored ivory box shown in Plate 60 with
the lid removed

Plate 62 Skeleton of a small child *in situ* in tomb 636 H.4, inside inlaid-shell box, and funerary jar

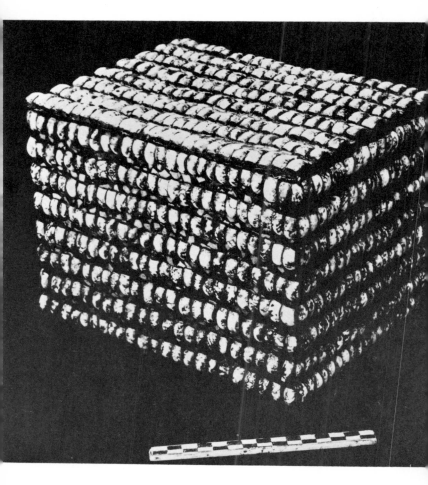

Plate 63   Restored inlaid-shell box shown in Plate 62

Plate 64   Wooden burial box found near tomb 668 H.5

Plate 65   Wooden burial box shown in Plate 64 with the
lid removed, containing the bones of a bird,
probably a hawk

1H.9

Plate 66   Pottery objects found in tomb 1 H.9, probably
shuttles and pegs used in looms

Plate 67   Piece of fine linen cloth

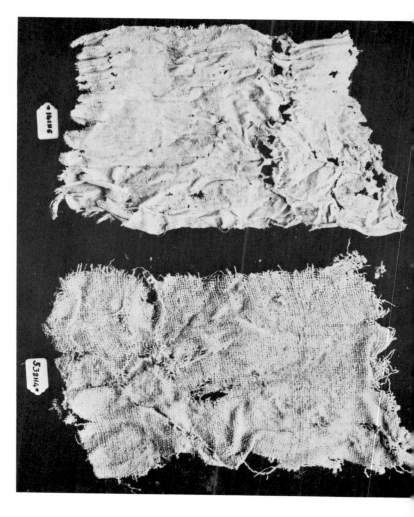

Plate 68 Pieces of thick, coarse linen cloth

Plate 69   Stela found in tomb 247 H.6 showing a figure
dressed in a long robe tied at the shoulder, seated
at a table surrounded by funerary offerings

Plate 70   Stela showing a woman seated at a table
surrounded by funerary offerings

150

Plate 71   Ivory comb with straw case found in tomb
621 H.5

Plate 72 Symbolic comb made of polished slate, found in
tomb 17 H.8

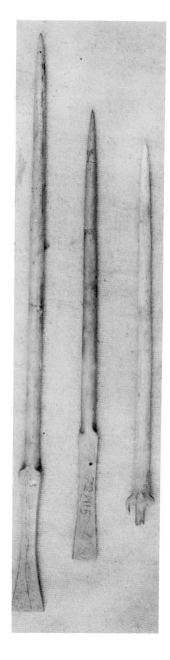

Plate 73
Selection of
ivory kohl sticks

Plate 74 Copper mirror with a wooden handle

Plate 75   Slate palette decorated with the ka and hieroglyphs denoting (left to right) prosperity,
life, happiness

6D9 4 11

Plate 76 Slate palette in the form of a fish, with eyes made
of shells

156

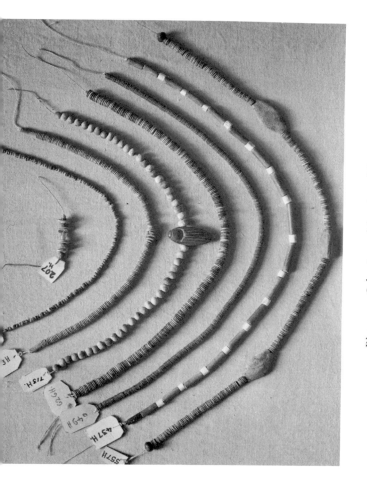

Plate 77 Selection of bead necklaces

157

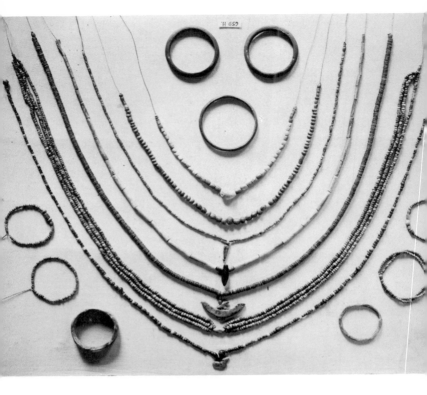

Plate 78 Necklaces and bracelets found in tomb 659 H.

158

Plate 79   Pectoral made of faïence beads found in tomb
337 H.3

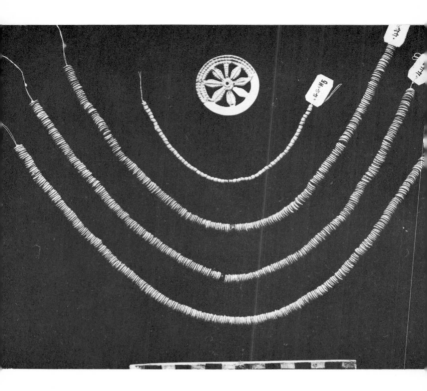

Plate 80   Four faïence necklaces and a wheel-shaped
pendant found in tomb 440 H.5

Plate 81   Detail of the eight-spoked wheel shown in Plate 80

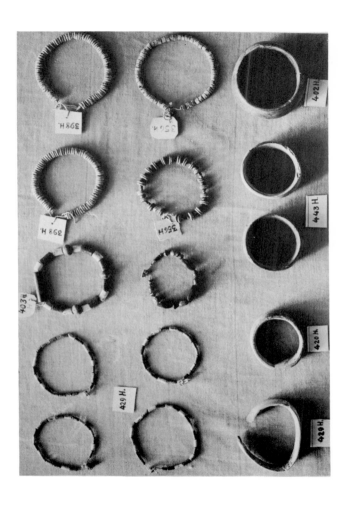

Plate 82   Selection of bracelets made of faïence, ivory, slate, and mother-of-pearl

162

Plate 83　Selection of slate bracelets

Plate 84   Ivory bracelets found on armbones in tomb 443 H.

Plate 85   Oval dolomite disks with holes bored at each end,
probably worn as bracelets

Plate 86 Four pottery granaries *in situ* in tomb 1502 H.2

Plate 87   Five mud-brick granaries near tomb 679 H.4

Plate 88　Ibex horns, the two upper horns broken and
mended in ancient times

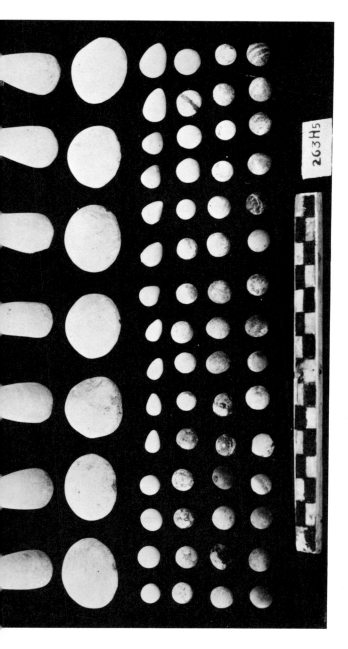

263 H5

Plate 89   Set of alabaster draughtsmen and beads found in
tomb 263 H5

Plate 90 Ivory pieces used in a game similar to chess

Plate 91   Name of King Aha carved on a fragment of an
alabaster vessel

Plate 92   Name of King Qaa carved on a fragment of slate

Plate 93   Name and portrait of Queen Neit-hetep carved
on an ivory fragment

173

Plate 94   Pottery-jar stopper bearing the name of a king
(probably Djer)

Plate 95   Cylindrical soapstone seal and its impression,
showing the representation of King Aha

Plate 96 Cylindrical hematite seal and its impression, found in tomb D. H.9

176

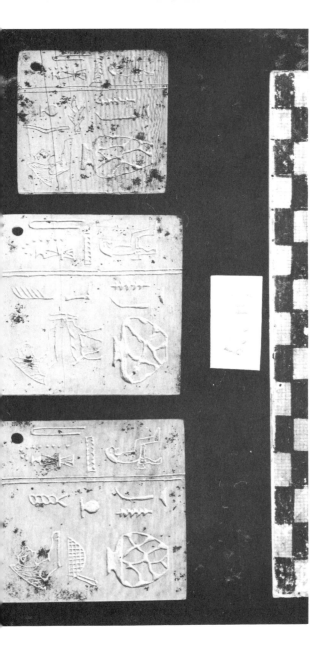

Plate 97 Ivory vase labels found in tomb 635 H.9, bearing the name of the owner, the contents of the vase, and a drawing of the vase

Plate 98 Inkholders with wells for red and black ink

Plate 99   Inkholder with lid, found in tomb 270 H.5

Plate 100   Inkholder shown in Plate 99 with the lid removed

Plate 101   Inkholder shown in Plates 99
and 100 *in situ* with skeleton
in tomb 270 H.5

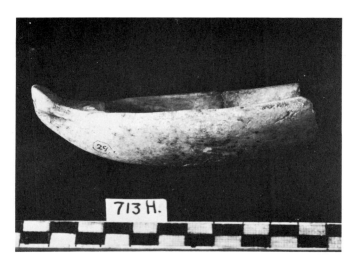

Plate 102 Model of a boat carved from ivory, found in
tomb 713 H.

Plate 103   Model of a boat carved from yellow limestone
in imitation of papyrus stalks

Plate 104 Model of a boat made of pottery

Plate 105   Wooden funerary boat *in situ* west of tomb
649 H.5

Plate 106   Wooden boat *in situ* north of tomb 575 H.5

Plate 107 Wooden boat *in situ* north of tomb 1216 H.9

Plate 108   Wooden boat *in situ* north of tomb 423 H.9

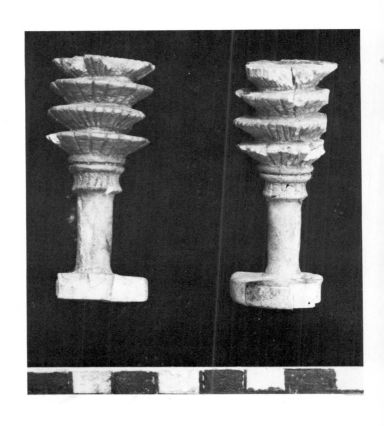

Plate 109   Two ivory symbols of Osiris as a fertility god,
carved to represent cypress trees with tied
branches

Plate 110 Ivory spoon and coffer lid bearing symbols of
Isis

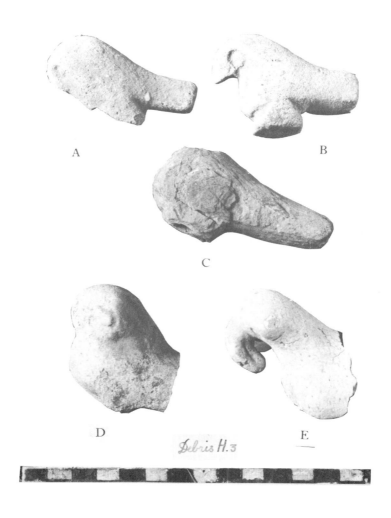

A

B

C

D

E

*Debris H.*3

Plate 111   Stone symbols of the falcon (A to D), representing Horus, and of the vulture (E), representing
Nekhbet

Plate 113
Copper emblem of a falcon
(symbol of Horus) crouching
on the symbol of Min

Plate 112
Symbols of the fertility god Min

Plate 114 Burial chamber of tomb 722 H.5 showing a skeleton in the fetal position, surrounded by funerary offerings

Plate 115   Coffin made of plant stems found in tomb 885 H.8

Plate 116   Grave (102 H.) without funerary objects

Plate 117   Burial chamber and magazine of tomb 116 H.4
with funerary objects

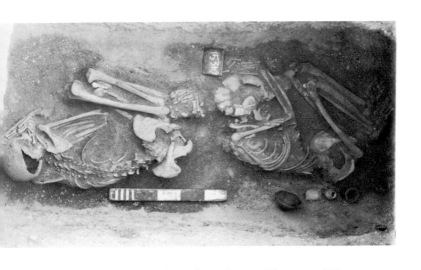

Plate 119   Burial chamber of tomb 153 H.9, containing
two skeletons

Plate 118   Burial chamber and four magazines of tomb
174 H.

Plate 120   Skeleton of a donkey *in situ* (53 H.10)

Plate 121   Skeleton of a dog and funerary objects in a coffin
in situ in tomb 421 H.3

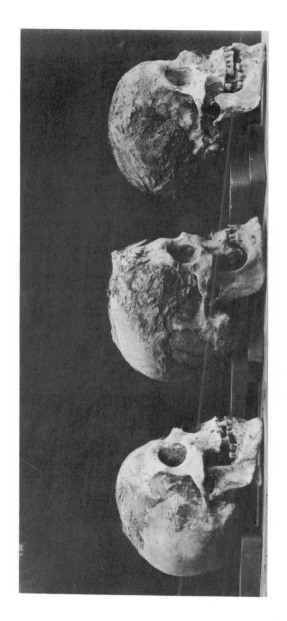

Plate 122   Three skulls with hair

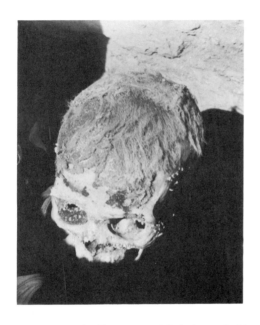

Plate 123   A skull *in situ* with hair and skin

Index

DATE DUE

GAYLORD   PRINTED IN U.S.A.

of name, 11, 14–16; baths at, 14; *see also* Iwnw

Helwan (Arab leader): 11, 14

Helwan necropolis: plundering of, 4–5, 20 n.; excavations at, 4–5, 9, 17–37, 46, 70–71, 73, 75–77, 80, 82–84; location of, 7, 9, *87;* Coptic monastery at, 14–16; use of limestone in, 24–37; graves in, 46, 74–75, *194, 198;* funerary barks in, 75; as cemetery of upper class, 82; *see also* cloth and clothing; crafts; Egyptians, ancient, pastimes of; First Dynasty; food; jewelry; kohl; Second Dynasty; tombs; writing and writing materials

Hemaka (noble): 75 & n.

Horus (god): 27–28, 73–74, *190;* union with Min, 74, *191*

Hunting and fishing: 42, 63–64, *168*

Isis (goddess): 45, 73–74, *189*

Ivory, used by Egyptians: 39, 43–45, 51, 53, 57, 63–66, 68, 70, 73–74; boxes made of, 43, 45–46, *138–42*

Iwnw: 9–11, 16; *see also* Helwan

Jars: *see* vases and jars, pottery

Jewelry: 39, 43, 45–46, 55, 57–58, 64, *157–65*

Junker, Hermann: 7, 9

Kha-sekhemui, King (Second Dynasty): 24, 36

Knives: 30–31, 39, 42–43, *126–28*

Kohl: 53

Limestone, in First Dynasty tombs: 18, 22, 24, 26, 28–29, 31–37, 39–43, 70, 75, 83, 97, *101–103, 113;* source of, 26; used in ointments, 55; transportation of, 69–70; *see also* tombs

Linen: *see* cloth and clothing

Lower Egypt, kingdom of: 9, 66–67, 84

Maadi, Egypt: 8, 11; excavations at, 8

Maasara, Egypt: 7

Memphis, Egypt: 9, 67

Min (god): 27–28, *191;* union with Horus, 74, *191*

Mirrors: 39, 43, 55

Mokattam Hills: 7, 26

Monastery, Coptic, at Helwan: 14–16; Byzantine origin of, 15

Mummies: 9

Narmer, King (First Dynasty): 6, 27, 82

Neit-hetep, Queen (First Dynasty): 66–67, *173*

Nekhbet (goddess): 28, 74, *190*

Neterimu, King (Second Dynasty): 82

Nile River: 7, 19, 26, 69, 71, 77; burial sites near, 7, 9, 14–15

Osiris (god): 73–74, *188*

Paint, in First Dynasty tombs: 22